resilience road

exploring your authentic life path

beth koritz, lpc

Aquarian Press

Saint Louis, Missouri

Copyright © 2019 by beth koritz.

beth koritz/Aquarian Press

koritzcc.com

*Names in this book were changed wherever the author shared personal details that were not solely hers to share.

Ordering Information:

Quantity sales. Special discounts are available on quantity purchases by corporations, associations, and others. For details, contact koritzcc.com.

resilience road/beth koritz. 1st ed.

978-0-9842182-9-5

This book is dedicated to:

My Two Tough Chiquitas

You are my Everything

Finding your authentic self is a journey without a final destination.

~beth koritz

Gratitude

First and foremost I want to thank my daughters, who have given me the gift of always wanting to strive to be the best me I can be. I love you both more than words can say. My journey would not have been as meaningful without you. To my parents, who have always loved and supported me unconditionally and have given me the example of what a long and happy marriage looks like. I could not have done this without you and I would not have wanted to. To my sister, who has had my back through every up and down, and been with me at every twist and turn. I sleep better each night knowing we would lay down our lives for each other. To my brother, who, because of our age difference, became so very important to me a little later in life. You have given me the gift of enjoying live music and all the amazing friends and fun that come with it. Many of my most cherished memories are thanks to you. To my brother- and sister-in-law, you are really my second brother and sister, and you both bring joy to my life in so many ways. To my extended family of aunts, uncles and cousins, who are always there for me. How lucky are we to have this family? To my grandmothers and great-grandmothers, who were such an integral part of the person I have become and such wonderful role models to have. To Michelle and Cousin Kate—this book would have never been completed without your generous help and patience. To Dr. Parks, who has been with me almost every step of the way. Thank you for always listening to me and trusting that I know my body.

Lastly, to my younger self for going through all of the challenges life threw at me so that my current self could learn to live a happy, authentic life.

-Much Love, beth

Things Have to Change

Dear Reader,

We are not on one continuously linear path from point A to point B. We are not born to be on a zip line, pointing our noses toward the only goal we'll ever see and then gripping the handles for dear life until we get there. The journey we are on changes just like the path in the forest erodes, fades, and deepens with the seasons.

As you read through this collection of stories and all the "*What the fuck?!?*" moments that I share, you may find it hard to believe that they all belong to one person. I promise you they do, along with many others that didn't make the cut. Despite the number of these moments, I am completely confident that I am now on the right path for *me* at this point in my life.

I am very aware that I said "at this point in my life." What often hangs people up—what really hung me up when I was on the wrong path but was too stubborn to get off of it until I felt I had no other choice—is the idea that once you've made a decision, it's a decision that you are stuck with for the rest of your life.

I believe that our lives are meant to be filled with joy and peace. If we don't give ourselves permission to take forks in the road, we may miss those moments.

I also believe it is easy to become complacent. We find safety in staying in the known even if the known makes us feel stuck and unhappy. We stay stuck all the time because the devil we know is better than the devil we don't know.

A ship is safe in harbor, but that's not what ships are for. I am certainly not here to say I've found the meaning of life, but I believe very strongly that whatever the meaning of life is, it requires us to venture out of our comfort zones and take some risks.

I see women and men in my practice who stay in relationships out of fear they will not meet someone else. There is truth to the adage that you have to be happy by yourself in order to make the best choices for you.

When you are comfortable in your own skin, with who you are, you are much more likely get out of a bad relationship, or a bad job, etc. You are much more likely to understand that you are better off being on your own than being with the wrong person or in the wrong place. Every day you remain in a situation that doesn't serve your greater good or allows you to stay true to your authentic self is another day that you miss the opportunity for the situation that is right for you.

What I'm saying is: you have to know who your authentic self is and then like that person. When I tell some clients that our work together will mean getting to know their authentic self, they'll respond, "I have no idea who that is." That's when I assure them that this is where they are going to figure it out. We will figure it out together.

It is possible to live your whole life without ever really listening to your inner voice letting *you* know who *you* are—and are not. It isn't because she hasn't been trying to tell you. That voice is there. It may be drowned out by the noise of checklists and drama, but it is there, whispering or screaming, desperate or resolved to be heard. Shhhhh. Listen...

As you think about your own life and your own resilience road you will likely realize you have had many *"What the fuck?!?"* moments of your own. I hope this book helps you develop your resilience road map to deal with those that have happened and those that have yet to happen. Go... Explore!

Happy Travels!

~beth

Map

Where's a Map
When You Need It?

I had been in the ICU for weeks waiting for this moment. Waiting was all I could do. I was paralyzed from the shoulders down and on life support, with a tube down my throat so I couldn't even talk. My own thoughts were the only thing available to me, and they weren't very cheery.

At times, a badass fighter would rise up inside of me, and in those moments I knew I was going to make it. I had kids to fight for. No way were my girls going to grow up without me. I could handle this. But that badass appeared only intermittently, and in her absence I was filled with dread. There were times I wasn't sure I was ever going to leave that room.

My medical team was finally going to pull the tube out of my throat. I'd be able to talk again. I could interact with my family, assure my kids it was going to be okay, start the long journey of recovery, and (first on my mind) share what I had been thinking about all of those days and nights lying immobile with nothing but my own thoughts to keep me company. I had been making plans.

1

The doctors told me not to talk for the first 24 hours after they removed the breathing tube. My throat was a raw mess. It felt like someone had lined my mouth with sandpaper. I took shallow breaths that stung, and rasped out words just above a whisper.

My husband walked into the hospital room to see me after they finished the procedure. He hadn't even made it all the way to the bed before I caught his eye and scratched out the words that had been bouncing around in my head with more and more fervor these past weeks.

"Things have to change," I said to him.

There was no way I was going to live the rest of my life—whether that was 10 days or 100 years—feeling the regret that I'd faced alone in that bed.

I'm getting a little ahead of myself here. That moment was a turning point, and this book is an exploration of the turn. Hopefully it can offer some guidance if you are facing a potential turn in your own life. But in order to understand the turn, you have to understand what came before it. Though I always had a free spirit inside of me, I had spent most of my life up to that point trying to be what other people wanted me to be: Thinner. Quieter. More reserved. More like everybody else.

Whether it was trying to be the perfect private school mom around my kids' classmates' parents or trying to squeeze into the right size jeans, I'd spent most of my years up to that point trying to become someone else, to mold myself into what I thought other people wanted to see when they looked at me. It wasn't until that moment in the hospital bed that I realized I was already the person I was supposed to be. But realizing who I really was wasn't enough to undo the years of bullshit that had been piled on top of me. That would take some unpacking; metaphorical and literal.

Things didn't all change at once, but that moment was the pivotal point for the rest of my life. My past and future hinged around it like halves of a book. Everything I had been and everything I would become were both there, open for interpretation. I had to look back into the story I'd already told about myself and pick out the pieces that were really true, really me. In the process, I had to discard my attachment to the versions of myself that I had put on only to please someone else or to meet some invisible expectation that I'd felt placed upon me. It was only with a clear sense of who I was and where I'd been that I could see the rest of the story unfolding in a way that would make me want to be in it. Living authentically in a life I could proudly call my own became my primary drive.

"Things have to change." I said the words to my husband, but I was really talking to myself, and it wouldn't be the last time I'd have to coax myself into a reset.

Full Speed Ahead

I am far from the only person who has found herself unexpectedly living a life she didn't want to be living. In most of the tales I've heard about such dissatisfaction, the person living the "wrong" life is able to look back and point to some obvious misstep, some mistake that took them astray, some poor decision that led them away from their true calling. It's like when you make a mistake while knitting. It might take you a minute of examination, but you can eventually find the error. Then you can unravel backwards and pick up where you left off. You might be frustrated and feel like you lost valuable time, but you can see where things went wrong and get the stitches back on track.

I've spent a lot of time thinking about how I got to that point, and there is no clear moment where I'd gone wrong. I had grown up with plenty of opportunities to choose the "right" paths, and I was a hard worker who took advantage of them. I wasn't in a position of dissatisfaction through laziness, lack of education, or even unfortunate circumstances beyond my control. While my life had its fair share of crises and dashes of tragedies, none had derailed me from a path toward a different life.

The truth of it is that the life I was living when I decided things needed to change was a life three decades in the making. It was the life that I was *supposed* to be living, and I had happily embraced the choices that I'd made that had gotten me there. When there were forks in the road, I chose the ones I thought I was supposed to choose, and I was certain I would attain what I was supposed to want: career, great guy, marriage, kids, dream house, eternal bliss. I had internalized societal expectations and the "right" path was laid out in front of me as clearly as the colorful tiles in the game of life. Check, check, check. Each step took me closer to the dream. I can't look back on my past self and fault her for the choices she made. She did everything she could with the tools she had and her expectations about the life she wanted. Don't get me wrong. I loved my life, my husband, and my children. My life was not a mistake; I just wasn't living it as my best authentic self. Not everything in my life was unhappy. I just wasn't living it on my own terms. I wasn't in my own skin. I was creating the person I was supposed to be instead of experiencing all of these joys as my real self.

The problem wasn't in the journey. The problem was that I had never stopped to question the destination. It wasn't that I had dropped a stitch. It was that I had been knitting someone else's pattern.

Road Closed Ahead

Dallas, our youngest daughter, was 4. We were spending the Friday before Memorial Day weekend in the hospital... again. As it turns out, many of my medical crises have happened around this holiday. But this time it wasn't for me. My husband, Daniel had been having stomach issues and had an appointment for an upper GI test. I took him to the appointment and brought along some needlepointing with the intention of relaxing while doing a little people watching. I sat on the floor of the hospital lobby and leaned against the wall. As I went to make the first stitch, my hands weren't doing what my brain told them to do. It was disorienting. There was no pain, no pang of a pinched nerve, no tingly pin pricks of numbness. They were moving. They just weren't moving the way I wanted them to move.

It's almost impossible to describe how weird that feels. My body suddenly felt very foreign to me. If I didn't have control over my movements, who did? What did?

I took a deep breath and tried to calm myself down. After a few minutes I picked up the needlepoint and tried to make another stitch. My fingers grasped the needle, but as I urged it downward into the canvas, it veered left, off to the side, missing contact entirely. Something was very wrong.

Should I call the doctor? I wondered. *Yes!* There was no answer, so I left a message and reasoned that if she got back to me quickly enough I could just run to her office while I was waiting for Daniel and get checked out. I didn't feel sick. Maybe I had some kind of damage to my hands.

I glanced at the clock to see how much longer Daniel had for his procedure. Men can be such babies when it comes to medical things. I didn't want to leave to run over to my doctor's office if he was almost finished, which he was. Daniel met me in the lobby, and we went across the street for some lunch. *The doctor's office is just a few blocks away*, I kept thinking. Something in my gut was telling me I needed to be seen. Fast. I still hadn't mentioned anything to Daniel. He was wrapped up in his own worries (which, it would turn out, were unfounded. He was fine.).

Later that day I took Daniel home to rest and picked Dallas up from preschool. While I was sitting in the carpool line, my phone rang. My doctor was calling back.

"If this weren't Friday afternoon of a holiday weekend," I began, "I wouldn't be bothering you with this," trying to downplay what I was feeling.

"If this weren't Friday afternoon of a holiday weekend, I'd be telling you to drive down here right now," she said. "But it is, so I expect to see you first thing Tuesday morning. Be here when we open, and if it gets any worse, call me and go to the emergency room." I felt comfortable following this advice because my doctor has always been a brilliant diagnostician and always trusted my instincts when it came to my health. I picked up my daughter and headed home. *Maybe things would be fine*, I thought, but I was starting to get scared.

My sister had just had her first baby four days earlier. She and her husband were bringing my niece home from the hospital that day, and we planned to go see her. Daniel and I decided to take the girls out for pizza first. I drove, and we pulled up to a pizza joint where we had to walk down a flight of steps to get inside.

As I approached the steps, I could tell I was getting worse. I wasn't walking right. It was like I was drunk, one foot going a little too far in front of me, the other dragging a little too slowly behind. My legs just weren't behaving themselves. I managed to make it down the stairs, but then one of the girls needed to go to the bathroom—back up the stairs.

"You have to take her," I said to Daniel. I knew I only had one more climb in me. That's when I finally told him what was going on, though I think it should have been pretty obvious by that point. Anyone who watched me get out of the car must have thought I had been driving drunk with my whole family in tow.

At my sister's house I was too afraid to hold my niece. I didn't want to drop her, and I didn't want to give her whatever it was I had. By now I was sure something was seriously wrong with me.

Is it a brain tumor? Do I have MS? I was panicking at the list of possibilities, none of them comforting. How could I go from being fine one second and not able to control my limbs the next?

I did what so many of us do when there are unanswerable questions to be tackled. I called my mom. I told her what was going on. "If I wake up in the middle

of the night and need to go to the ER, can you take me?"
I didn't have a plan for what to do with the kids in the
morning, but at least Daniel had already taken this
Saturday off—the first Saturday in four years he'd be at
home—because he wanted to enjoy the holiday weekend.

That night I tossed and turned as I tried to sleep.
Whenever I turned over, my limbs lagged behind,
dragging themselves like debris clinging to the back of a
boat. When they finally caught up to my body, it would
wake me with a jolt. When I woke the next morning,
Daniel was in the adjoining sitting room watching
cartoons with the girls. "Daniel," I called out. "I'm going
to try to get up, but I want you next to me in case I can't
stand."

I threw my legs over the side of the bed and sat there
for a second. As I shifted my weight down to try to stand,
my legs crumpled beneath me. Daniel caught me as I
lurched forward. I was completely helpless to control my
unresponsive body. He guided me back onto the bed, and
I laid there, awash in terror.

The girls were only a few feet away, and I didn't want
them to know how scared I was. I called my mom and
asked her to come get me because I didn't want them to
see me leave in an ambulance. This was not the first or
last time I didn't use an ambulance when I should have.
In every case it was a combination of not wanting to call
attention to myself and not wanting to admit the
seriousness of the situation. But more about that later.

Then I called my doctor. "Go to the ER," she said,
adding that as soon as she got off the phone with me she
would call a neurologist. The neurologist was on his way
to the golf course, but he pulled off the highway and
headed back to the hospital to meet me.

My mom arrived and came to the bedroom. I hollered, "Goodbye!" to my kids, not knowing when I would see them again. I didn't think I could get through hugging and kissing them goodbye without crying and frightening them. Mom was on one side and Daniel on the other as they shuffled me—legs dragging against the ground—to the car. By the time we got the ER I had nothing left. I couldn't move. A security guard had to scoop me up like a child and place me in the wheelchair, arranging my legs as he sat me down.

The nurse asked me to move from the wheelchair to a table.

I tried to push myself up and nothing happened. "I can't move my legs," I said. "They aren't working. You're going to have to help me." She wasn't paying attention to me. I started to fall between the chair and the table because she was offering only support rather than holding on to me. As I toppled forward, the nurse let out a gasp and caught me just before I hit the ground. As she pushed me onto the table, the neurologist arrived.

Right away I was put on a gurney and wheeled away for an electromyography (EMG). It was truly a ghoulish experience. I was on a gurney with an orderly navigating the way. The elevator descended into the bowels of the hospital. The ubiquitous hospital pastel faded away as we emerged into a corridor of unpainted cinderblocks. Air conditioning and plumbing pipes loomed over my head, the only things I could see as I was stuck flat on my back. I could hear the noises of a kitchen. *This isn't a medical floor!* I thought in a panic. There wasn't another human being in sight, and I couldn't move my body. *This guy could do anything to me down here!* It was humbling (not to mention terrifying!) to find out what it felt like to have zero defenses. To have nothing. *No one could hear me yell. How long would it take someone to find me? What kind of tests do you do down here?*

The stage was set for a Frankenstein scene. I was wheeled into a room with one doctor and a machine, but no nurses or support staff. For the EMG, the doctor sticks an electrode into your muscle before running an electric current through it to shock your muscle and measure its response.

It is hell.

I couldn't move, and it wasn't enough for the doctor to test one leg. He had to test each individual muscle in each leg. It just didn't stop. "This is a torture device," I mumbled between painful jolts to my immobile legs. "This was invented by the Nazis." I may not have had the ability to move, but I had full feeling in my entire body. I felt everything. This test went on for close to an hour.

Afterwards, I was wheeled back to the land of the living and placed in a room with a roommate I never saw. I was on the inside part of the room, near the window, and my roommate was gone when the orderly wheeled me past her bed. Once he pulled the curtain, I was immobile on my own side of the room.

Daniel had found someone to watch the kids at home and was there in the room with me. Someone came in to give me a spinal tap, rolling me on to my side because I couldn't do it on my own. The needle hit a nerve, and I was screaming in pain.

"Hang in there. Hang in there. We're going to get it."

Finally, the technician tapped and was getting fluid, but the needle was on a nerve the whole time. Sparks of pain shot down my leg. Daniel couldn't handle my screaming, so he scurried to the hall to wait it out. As soon as the needle was pulled out, the pain stopped. I felt like I had been through a battle.

"I don't know what they did to you," a disembodied voice floated from the other side of the curtain, "but they sure as hell better not do it to me!"

Apparently, my roommate had returned.

Soon after, the neurologist came in. "You have Guillain-Barré Syndrome," he said. "The good news is it won't kill you, but the way it works is that it has to get as bad as it's going to get, and then you'll come back. But everybody's worst point is different, so we don't know how much paralysis you'll have. There's a treatment we can do called plasmapheresis. It will remove certain antibodies from your plasma that are contributing to your immune system's attack on the peripheral nerves. You'll have three to five of these treatments over time. Also, the muscles around your lungs are going to get compromised soon, so we're going to intubate you and put you on a ventilator. Probably tomorrow we'll put you in the ICU. If you want to see your kids before you go in, have someone bring them now. They won't be able to see you once you're in the ICU."

I flashed back to the times I'd been in this hospital, when I gave birth to my girls. Who knew that only a few years later I would be thinking I might be saying goodbye to them for the last time?

I asked my mother to have the babysitter bring them in, and then I was wheeled out again to have a port (to deliver medicine) inserted under my right clavicle. When I got back from the procedure, the kids were at the hospital. Dallas was running a little fever, so there was a big deal being made over whether or not she'd be allowed to see me. Finally, the doctors said she could come in if she wore a mask. She had just turned 4. How are you going to get a 4-year-old to keep a mask on? We decided that our best shot was to have everyone wear a mask so she didn't feel singled out.

I tried to put on a smile and look optimistic. I didn't want them to think about my being immobile and sick. I told them I'd be coming home soon after the doctors made me better. "You might not see me for a while."

I tried to sound reassuring, but I was fighting back fear and tears. The doctor said this wouldn't kill me, but I wasn't sure I could believe him. I was terrified. My girls were only 4 and 7. How can you get kids that young to understand something so big?

That evening I got my first plasmapheresis treatment. Using the port that had been inserted earlier, blood was taken out of my body, run through a machine that spun the plasma out and replaced it with synthetic plasma and then moved it back into my body. I had to do this long enough to get all of my blood scrubbed. During the treatment, there was a risk that my blood pressure could dip dangerously low. I was shivering—freezing. Whenever the beeping machine determined my blood pressure was too low, a nurse would pause the procedure and place a Tums under my tongue to dissolve. Once my blood pressure was back up, the nurse would put another warm blanket over my freezing body and start again. This went on for five hours. I couldn't sleep because she had to monitor how I was responding, so I was awake and aware the entire time. I never knew something could be simultaneously so boring and so terrifying.

I was finally back in my room around midnight.

What a day!

The next morning I was moved to the ICU. The paralysis had been slowly creeping over my body like a bank of storm clouds rolling in.

I was in the Neuro ICU. My parents mentioned they had been in the waiting room with another set of parents who were there for their daughter who had fallen while roller blading without a helmet in Forest Park. It turned out this woman had a child in Dallas's class. Our parents had been chatting enough to figure out their grandchildren were classmates. So in a class of 24 children, two of them had moms in the Neuro ICU. I later learned the school brought social workers in on Tuesday to help Dallas, the other mom's son, and the rest of the kids process what was going on.

Guillain-Barré Syndrome (GBS) is an autoimmune disease named after two French doctors. It destroys the myelin sheath around nerves, much like multiple sclerosis. Once the sheath is destroyed, the muscle those nerves controlled becomes paralyzed. Unlike MS, the sheath can regenerate itself in a GBS patient. Some people have a version so mild that it's never even diagnosed. They might just get tingly hands that eventually stop tingling. Other people, like me, become fully paralyzed.

By Tuesday, the paralysis had moved far enough up my body that the doctors were concerned about my ability to breathe. I was intubated and put on life support. As I was lying there, unable to move and now unable to talk, I was scared that I was going to die. *I'm going to do this*, I told myself. *I'm going to live.*

I could feel my grandma's spirit behind my left shoulder like an angel, a weighted, comforting presence that seemed to be cheering on my silent pep talk. *I'm going to do this. I'm going to do this. I'm going to live for my kids. I'm going to do this, but I'm only going to do it once. There's no way I'm going through this hell again.* I'm sure if I was faced with the same diagnosis today, I'd say, *Fuck that. I got through it once. I'll get through it again.* But at the time, I could only manage to gather the energy to fight by telling myself I'd never have to do it again.

I also kept thinking I was so glad my grandmother wasn't alive to see me like this. *It would kill her,* I thought. She had been the matriarch of our family, and I was the oldest of her eight grandchildren. We were very close. She would always tell me: "I'm not really supposed to have favorites, but you're my favorite." We spent a lot of precious time together. She was, and continues to be, a guiding force in my life.

Whenever I have a big decision to make—or for that matter, a small decision—I ask myself what she would think about it. Most of my lessons on manners, how men should treat women, and how to be a "lady" come from her. Ironically, she had died in that very hospital a few years before. The day I was admitted was her wedding anniversary. I felt very connected to her at that time.

There's nothing to do when you're on life support. No TV, no distractions. I was heavily sedated because I kept trying to fight the intubation tube. All I had time to do was think. And then, on top of everything else, I contracted pneumonia.

Thanks to the pneumonia, I had to be treated by a respiratory therapist twice a day, who would come in and pound on my chest and back. It's hard to find any humor in a situation like that, especially when you're frozen and unable to respond. It was like a kid pounding on a drum set as you listened with tortured ears and gritted through clenched teeth. "That's great honey. Thanks for that. Are you *done yet?!*"

I was on life support for 10 days. Occasionally I would see people pass by and stop in the doorway. I had family members who worked in the hospital, and they'd stop by to check on me, but their presence was a haze. I didn't really overhear much or have anything to focus on except my own thoughts. That solitude, that intensity, turned it into a life-changing experience.

Life's short; make the most of it. *Before, this was something I would have thought to see in needlepoint on a throw pillow, some bullshit that you say without giving it any weight or meaning. But not anymore. Now it was ingrained in my very soul, and it was fast becoming my philosophy, the way I was going to live my life from now on. I would live for me.*

After the doctors removed the intubation tube, they told me not to talk for 24 hours. But I couldn't wait. As soon as I saw my husband, the first words out of my mouth were "Things have to change." I don't think he quite understood just what that would mean for our lives at the time. But I did and I meant what I said. First, though, I had some recovering to do.

beth koritz

Do not be misled by what you see around you, or be influenced by what you see. You live in a world which is a playground of illusion, full of false paths, false values and false ideals. But you are not part of that world.

~Sai Baba

Home Away From Home

As I look back on the defining moments of my life, I realize that a lot of them have a place in common: Camp Sabra, a Jewish sleep-away camp at the Lake of the Ozarks. It's still thriving to this day. I spent 14 summers there. While not all of my experiences at Camp Sabra were positive, they were all formative. It is a place that represents growth and transformation in my life, and it weaves itself in and out of my story.

I grew up at Camp Sabra. At 7 years old, I went for three weeks. I was the youngest camper there—that's a long time to be away from home for someone so young. Nowadays it's unheard of. A lot of the other girls were homesick and cried at night because they missed their parents. I wasn't really homesick, but I felt like I was supposed to be because everybody else was. All around me girls were whining and crying for their parents. I wondered what was wrong with them, but I pretended to be sad so I wouldn't stand out. This is my first actual memory of pretending to be something that I wasn't just to fit in.

After that first year, I attended camp four weeks during every summer of my childhood. I was in the equestrian program the first year it was offered. We would wake up early every morning and walk the half-mile to the stables where we would feed our horses before walking back for breakfast. I had a wonderful gray mare named Becky. Together Becky and I had many good and not-so-good times that summer.

I had grown up riding horses at my grandparents' farm, where they bred thoroughbreds, and I had a quarter horse named Chippies. I named her after my favorite cereal, Rice Krispies. But at the age of 6 the word Krispies came out as Chippies. Chippies and I were in a few western show competitions where we won ribbons that I thought were amazing.

With Becky that summer, I learned how to stand on a saddle and how to groom. We even had an overnight trip on horseback! On that overnight we were riding through a creek bed with branches arching overhead. One of the branches had a hornet's nest on it. A group leader saw it and warned us all to duck low. Everyone bent forward and cleared the branch except for one person near the back of the group who must have bent backward. The brim of their riding helmet hit the hornet's nest.

The next thing we knew, the horses were freaking out and flying in every direction. The hornets were stinging every living thing—horse and human. The horses just took off. I remember being so startled that I dropped the reins. My horse was flying through the woods, trees and thickets flying past in a blur. I was hanging on to the saddle horn for dear life and we were all getting farther and farther from each other. I got stung six times, so my body was hurting, but I kept trying to cling to this petrified horse. When we finally got the horses calmed down and found each other again, we moped back to the campsite and spent the next hour making mud packs for our stings. Somewhere we had heard it would dull the pain. Like I said, camp was memorable.

During this time I got plenty of opportunities to travel and explore. The following year, when I was 12, we were all looking forward to a five-day camping trip to Arkansas. But a week before the camping trip, I got a big surprise...

One night the camp had organized a social for my age group so we could hang out on our own in the woods. The unit leaders had strung lights to create an outdoor party zone where we could socialize and dance. After dinner, around nine o'clock, we all went back to the cabins to change clothes for the social. My shoes were underneath a tree outside the cabin. As I went out to get them, I felt a sting on my neck that hurt bad—like I'd been hit with a baseball bat in my neck bad. I had no idea what it was, but the pain lessened pretty quickly, so I went ahead and got dressed and went to the social.

Within half an hour I was feeling horrible and told my unit leader I needed to go back and lie down. The next thing I knew, it was the middle of the night and my unit director (who I guess had been checking on me—I must have passed out) was hovering over me. He was a Shaliach (an emissary) from Israel and a reporter for the *Jerusalem Post* who was spending a year working at the local Jewish Community Center. He was shaking me awake. He literally scooped me out of bed and carried me to the infirmary. What I didn't know was that while I was passed out I had a raging fever and my neck had become increasingly swollen. Apparently, at that point, they called my parents, who got in their van at 5 o'clock in the morning and drove down to camp.

When they woke me again, around breakfast time, they told me that my parents were there to pick me up and take me home. My siblings told me later it was weird for them when they got to the dining hall for breakfast because our parents were there and they had no idea why. (This was the first time I left camp in a van, crying out in pain at every bump in the road. Little did I know I would repeat this whole experience with eerie similarity in the exact same place nearly four decades later.)

It was pretty awful. Later, when doctors looked at the bite, they said it must have been a brown recluse spider. My neck continued to swell until it expanded beyond my jaw line. I looked like I was wearing one of those travel pillows under my skin!

When my parents came to pick me up, there was talk of taking me to a hospital. But I had two family members who were doctors, so they ultimately decided to treat me at home, where they watched my fever and started counting down the hours. If the fever didn't break I would have needed to be hospitalized for fear of renal failure. This was the first time in my life that I was completely incapacitated, and the memories linger. I was lying there feeling helpless, waiting for other people to decide what needed to be done with me. Unfortunately, it wouldn't be the last time I would feel this way.

After four days the fever broke and the wound started to heal up. My designated time at camp wasn't over yet, so I went right back to finish up the summer with five days roughing it in Arkansas. And by "went right back," I mean that my parents sent 12-year-old me *by myself* on a Greyhound bus. I ended up swinging from helpless physical incapacitation like I'd never known before to more freedom than I had ever been given all in a matter of days. It was dizzying.

It was my first traumatic experience where the support of my family and my self-determination and focus on the positive propelled me back into the saddle, so to speak.

The camp trips got progressively more involved as I got older, including a 10-day trip to Colorado one year and a two-week trip to Canada the following year. When I was 15, as part of the oldest group of campers, I went to Israel for six weeks.

This was the year Mount Sinai was slated to be returned to Egypt, so we knew we would be one of the last groups to climb it in Israel. That climb is the site of one of my favorite pictures of myself. I'm kicked back on a rock on top of Mount Sinai! It's one of the few images I have of myself from my youth where I felt beautiful.

We stayed on a kibbutz for five days and worked in the cotton fields for eight hours a day. After one of those days of work I got heat stroke. I came back and slept for 24 hours, losing an entire day of my trip.

People always ask me if I felt safe in Israel. I felt safer there than anywhere. There were soldiers carrying Uzis all around me. While that may make some uncomfortable, it had me feeling very safe.

I had an old camp friend who was going to be in Israel at the same time I was there, so we decided to try to meet up. All the Americans knew about a pizza parlor called Richie's in Tel Aviv. An entire wall was dedicated for people to post notes telling where and when to meet. My friend and I had agreed that whoever got there first would leave a post at Richie's.

When I got to Richie's, I scanned the bulletin board and didn't see anything from my friend, so I left her a note and headed out of the restaurant. I was not five yards down the sidewalk when my friend came running up to me screeching and jumping up and down. We'd ended up at Richie's mere minutes apart.

"Shh! Shh!" I tried to get her to calm down because she was drawing a lot of attention to us. I've never liked being the center of attention, and I like it even less when the audience is made up of heavily armed soldiers always on the alert for an attack! You don't jump around and scream like that in the streets in Israel. It wasn't until she noticed the soldiers running toward us to see what was going on that she stopped screaming.

Those Israeli boys sure loved us American girls! One of them might have loved this American girl a little too much. He was a boy named Gidon, who took me to the River Jordan. I'd heard so many amazing stories that made the river out to be such a massive force, something mythical even. It was nothing but a trickle. I could literally step over it in a single step. But my experience with Gidon was very romantic for my teenage self. He sent me letters after I got back home, professing his undying love and saying he couldn't live without me. My parents rolled their eyes. "He's trying to get a visa!" That knocked what I perceived as romance into left field!

The trip came to an end. I had racked up a lot of new experiences and memories. I had two weeks back at camp as a camper. Then, overnight, I became a staff member. The same people who had been supervising me one day became my co-workers the next. Suddenly I was going out at night with my camp counselors. I wondered where I fit. What was my place? I was trapped somewhere between childhood and adulthood, excited about my new responsibilities but not quite feeling comfortable with handling them on my own.

At that time a group rented out the entire camp for two weeks to provide 250 African-American inner-city kids a summer camp experience. While the group brought its own counseling staff, a handful of us Sabra staff stayed to run the camp activities: swimming, canoeing, sailing, etc. Although we did not have much interaction with the kids, the mix presented a bit of a culture clash and was fraught with tension. I was the only camp-employed female staff member, which meant I was the only white person living in the girls' village.

One night there was an odd scraping sound, and some of the girls looked out their cabin window and saw a white man who obviously didn't belong there. They were scared. Even though nothing happened, they suspected the worst intentions.

The next morning the group's staff got together and decided that its men would patrol the girls' village to keep it safe. That night as I was walking back from the shower house, four or five of the men approached me.

As I tried to walk away, one of them grabbed my arm and held me so tightly he left bruises. They were all yelling at me because they thought that the man in the village could have only been there to see me. If a white guy was creeping around, he must have been associated with the only white girl, they reasoned. I knew just as much about the man and his intentions as they did—that is, nothing! They said he had no business being there and if they saw him again, they were going to "take care" of both of us. The entire confrontation was very threatening and scary. I yanked away and ran straight to the director's office, shaking like a leaf.

He moved me out of the village immediately and put me in the swim cabin, isolated from everyone. Up until this point camp was a place where I was comfortable being me. I had felt safe there in every way.

It was a very tense time, and I imagine everyone was relieved when the two weeks were up.

As soon as the group pulled out of camp, the remaining Sabra staff decided to go swimming. As we cut across the swim cove over the footbridge, someone looked out into the lake.

"What is that?"

It was my trunk! As a final act of anger, someone had broken into my cabin and thrown my footlocker in the lake. Another half hour and it would have been completely submerged and out of sight forever. Some of the guys took a boat out and ran a pole through the trunk handle to lift it out of the water. We had to spread all my belongings across the deck to dry.

I hadn't even been home yet. I went straight from Israel to working at the camp, so all my clothes and all the presents I had brought back with me were in that trunk. Everything was soaked. This was an act of hatred against me—and it happened in my safe place. I felt angry and vulnerable at the same time. This was personal. Even though at the age of 15 I didn't have the skills to process this display of hatred, it did not keep me from having fun with my friends as all of my belongings were laid around us drying.

If transitioning from camper to staff was a symbolic switch from childhood to adulthood, there was one lesson that I learned that summer:

Adulthood was going to be complicated!

beth koritz

Every day is a journey and the journey itself is home.

~Matsuo Basho

Detour Ahead

The summer after I graduated high school was my time to spread my wings and revel in some independence before the new boundaries and responsibilities of college. Looking back, I realize that while I wasn't being totally true to myself, I was using this as a time to explore who I really was without the limitations of being who I "should be." I was meeting new people I hadn't been exposed to in school, trying new things and pushing limits.

Then my fun summer, my last big hoorah, was cut short because I got mononucleosis. The glands in my neck swelled up so far that I couldn't even turn my head! It was miserable! This was the second time that illness truly incapacitated me.

It was only two weeks before leaving for the Hotel and Restaurant Management program at Denver University (DU) and I was afraid I wouldn't be well enough to go on time. Nothing like needing to fit in and thinking that it was going to all start without me.

I improved enough that I was allowed to go, but I wasn't back to normal. I had two rules to live by; no lifting anything over 10 pounds, and no alcohol for *six months!* Talk about putting a damper on the traditional college experience!

My father drove from St. Louis to Denver with me and all my stuff packed into his car. The night before move-in we stayed at a hotel near campus, and went to the bar, which had a live band. While Dad and I were dancing, the band dedicated its next song "to this lovely couple on the dance floor."

I was mortified! My dad has always looked super young for his age and my parents had me when they were only 22, but still! I was 17 and on my way to my first year of college. I was ready to be seen as an adult, but that was a little much!

The next day as I sat at my dorm room window watching my dad walk away, I was still sick. I felt like crap. My body ached, and I didn't know a single person on the entire campus. I was watching the last link to my childhood walk away, and tears were rolling down my cheeks. I felt so alone.

I hated sharing 150 square feet with a stranger. I've always treasured my space and alone time. Then and throughout my life, having solitary space and time has always been important to me. I just hadn't yet made the connection to how important it was to my ability to be resilient.

With a lot of creativity and convincing I finagled a way to have a private room, but it was going to cost an extra $100 a month. My parents said it was fine for me to live alone, but that extra charge was my responsibility. Fine. I took the midnight to 8 a.m. shift at the front desk of the dorm. I would ask the person replacing me to come a few minutes early so that I could dash straight from the desk to my 8 o'clock class. It was absolutely exhausting, and there were times when I dozed off in class because I couldn't doze off at work. I was determined to keep that single room, though. Looking back through my life, I can now see that I've gotten everything I've wanted through determination and perseverance. If something I want means enough to me, I will figure out a way and work hard enough to get it!

I became friends with a junior named Dawn who was living alone in another room on our floor. Even though I was only a freshman, we became very close friends.

Like me, Dawn was a little on the outside of the social totem pole. She didn't care about cliques and didn't need to run in the most popular circles. That made it easy to be her friend. Everyone else she hung out with were guys, but they were nice guys, the kind you'd want to be friends with.

One of those friends from her hometown was a hostage during the Iranian hostage crisis. The crisis was still ongoing during my freshman year, and she was wrapped up in the news. Consequently, I became wrapped up in it, too. When it ended on January 20, 1981, her friend, Billy, was finally coming home. My 18th birthday was February 6. Billy hadn't even been home two weeks when he and Dawn took me out for my first legal drink (Colorado was a 3.2 state, so the legal drinking age was 18).

Billy was pretty famous at that point. Everyone kept crowding around him, asking to buy him a drink. Strangers came up from all around.

It was a weird moment for me. We were out for *my* birthday, but I didn't even know this guy and here he was with a flock of people around him. My birthday celebration had the feel of a celebrity entourage, but I was on the outside. It was like I was an integral part of an important group, but at the same time I wasn't really part of it at all. Once again I was in a situation where I felt like I didn't fit in.

During my sophomore year, Dawn and I decided to rent an off-campus apartment together. I was dirt poor. My meals were often popcorn and Kool-Aid because Kool-Aid at least added some flavor to the popcorn. This is when I got really creative with ramen. Some days, all I ate was ramen. A splurge was running up to Safeway for a sandwich at the deli counter. It was clear: I needed money, so I worked on getting a job.

I had my car with me by this time, so I could cast a wider net in my job search. There was a new restaurant called People's opening a couple of miles from campus. It was a brand-new dining concept: they offered not just a salad bar, but also a *food* bar. It was family-oriented and known for its 20-pound block of cheese on the bar. I got a job as a hostess and hostess trainer for the opening crew.

I was making the most of this year with classes, work, and making an effort to still have fun.

I've never been able to get into the athletic scene. At DU, skiing was huge. Everyone did it. Everyone, that is, except me. I don't have an athletic bone in my body, and nothing was appealing about strapping some boards on my feet and hurtling myself down the side of a cold mountain.

One night I was talking to the bartender at a local bar. It came up that I had never been skiing, and he was completely taken aback, as if I told him I'd never heard music before.

"Well, I'm going to teach you!" he heroically announced. "I'm taking you skiing tomorrow."

I said okay because I wanted to fit into the scene there. It also didn't hurt that he was really cute.

The next morning we met to drive to Keystone, stopping at a ski rental place because I had no gear of my own. In fact, I showed up wearing blue jeans, which should be enough to tell you exactly what my experience level was. We got skis, boots, and bindings, and headed into the mountains.

As I was putting on my skis, I heard him mutter, "Should we try the bunny slope first?" Before I could answer him ("Yes! We should definitely try the bunny slope first! I've never done this before!"), he answered himself. "Nah. Let's just go for it!" The next thing I knew, I was on a chair lift. (Have I mentioned I am terrified of heights?) I didn't know how to get off the thing. It's not as intuitive as you might think. I just sort of pushed myself off the seat and I fell. Hard. On my ass. Boom. Welcome to skiing.

He lifted me up, and we went a few feet. He gave me the basic overview of how to ski. "Keep your skis straight like French fries until you want to turn, and then you make them like a pizza." That's all he gave me to go on. "Okay," he said. "Let's go!"

It was terrifying. My body was tensed up from head to toe. On the rare instances where I got a little momentum and started moving smoothly and quickly, I got scared and intentionally fell to the ground so I didn't go too fast.

My rented bindings didn't fit my skis properly, so ice kept building up on the bottom of my boots. Every time I fell—and I fell *a lot*—I would stand up, and ice would layer beneath the sole of my boot so I couldn't click the boot back down in the binding. A few times, my date would take his ski pole and chip away at the ice so that I could get my ski back on, but I could tell he was getting bored with this slow progress. After about 45 minutes, he said, "Okay, I'll see you at the bottom."

And then I was alone.

I had no idea what I was doing. I didn't even know how to read the colored markers to figure out which path would kill me and which one would merely leave me tumbling and bruised. I just knew that I had to get to the bottom, and I damned sure was not going to make a scene up there and draw attention to myself by flailing around and asking for help. So I just kept moving downhill.

Slide. Fall. Slide. Fall. I was getting wetter and wetter. My jeans had pretty much turned completely white, I guess from the chemicals in the artificial snow. Another 45 minutes passed, and I was still far up the mountain. Every muscle in my body was screaming. Even though I was trying to blend in and not draw attention to myself, it was obvious I didn't belong there.

Sometimes nice people would take pity on me and help me a little before deciding they had done enough of a good deed and move on. About three hours into this ordeal I fell for what had to be the thousandth time, but this time I couldn't get up. I had nothing left. No energy. No muscles. Nothing to give.

I started praying: "God, if you will just get me off of this godforsaken mountain, I promise I will never, ever do this again." I got to the bottom four hours after I had started. This was a trip that took real skiers 25 minutes at the most.

Years later, I ended up marrying a man whose family had a condo in Vail, Colorado, where everyone was athletic and went skiing all the time. But I kept my promise to God. I never put on another pair of skis (much to my in-laws' dismay). The first time I went skiing it was because I wanted so badly to fit in. By this time I had grown enough that I was comfortable (not really, but I did it anyway) standing my ground and not relenting just to fit in.

Despite my efforts to balance a full life as a college student, things came to a head at the end of that summer after the school semester was finished. I was trying to be everything. I was working full-time at the restaurant and taking three classes at the community college to get ahead on cheap credits that would transfer to DU.

When classes ended at the community college, I had a one-week window before classes started back up at Denver University. It hit me all at once.

I was completely, utterly exhausted. I called my mom and had a crying breakdown on the phone. Hearing her voice always does that to me. It's like I bottle everything up, and knowing that she's listening gives me permission to unload. I wasn't ready for school to start. I needed a real break! This may have been the first time the Universe was shouting at me to slow down, and giving me physical reasons to make sure I did.

I was so overwhelmed and fatigued that I ended up moving back to St. Louis. I told myself it would just be for a little break, but I ended up quitting school.

I've always told my kids not to take summer school classes. That break is hugely important and exists for a reason. We need some space to clear our heads and let ourselves rest for a minute. Eighteen- and nineteen-year-olds aren't built to hold up under that kind of stress.

I even encouraged my younger daughter to drop some classes and take an extra semester to finish school. She is an artist, and those studio hours were long and exhausting. I kept telling her it would cost the same to do it in five years as it would to do it in four. Life is not a race. Take your time and enjoy it to the end with some energy left. I was hoping to impart the lesson I learned the hard way.

After I left school I went back to my parents' house. It's not easy to go from having your own apartment to sleeping in your childhood bedroom. It was a blow to my ego and my sense of independence. Suddenly I wasn't as grown-up as I'd thought I was.

I needed to get a job.

Since I had been working on a degree in Hotel and Restaurant Management at DU, I decided to find work related to that. I started working at the front desk of a hotel, and it was fun. I worked my way up to front desk manager. I remember having to go by Elizabeth there because they already had a Beth working the desk, and I thought it would be easier on everyone if I just went by the longer name. Here was a place where nobody knew me and I could continue developing the real me with no outside pressure or anybody's preconceived notion about who Beth was. Elizabeth was free to do all kinds of things Beth wouldn't have done. This is when my life began to revolve around music. My work friends and I would go dancing most nights when our shift ended at 11 p.m. Many entertainers performing at the nearby venue stayed at the hotel and I was able to enjoy many of their shows.

I worked there for about two years and while I really enjoyed the people I worked with, I knew I didn't want to spend my life working behind that desk. This wasn't the career for me.

Realizing that I was still no closer to my "real" adulthood than I had been before, I was starting to feel like I wasn't going to find a place where I fit career-wise. I wasn't ticking off the boxes on my internal checklist. You know that list—the one society tells us we are supposed to have to have the "right" life. This was a holding pattern, and I was keenly aware that I was staying stuck instead of moving forward.

It wasn't that I was bad at the work. By all measures, I was on a path to success. I was getting promoted. I was making friends. But I felt like I was wearing someone else's life, that I'd stepped into a role I wasn't supposed to play.

At this point I had been out of school for a few years, and my mom could tell I was drifting. She suggested that I talk to a friend of hers who was Dean of the Adult Learning Program at Lindenwood University. I wasn't sure about it.

"Just go meet her," my mom said. "What do you have to lose?" I decided she was right and I would at least see what my options were. It occurs to me now that I was already on the path of not passing up any opportunity that felt right.

The meeting went really well. Not only could I transfer all of my credits from DU, the community college in Denver, and from the courses I had taken when I got back to St. Louis, but they'd also give me credit for my life experience. It seemed too good to pass up.

I changed my major to Communications, and I got a B.S. instead of a B.A., which was typical for a Communications major. I wanted my education to be more business oriented. Counting up all of my semesters in school, I ended up doing a four-year degree in three and a half years—they were just a little more spaced out than most students.

I went to school full-time while working at the hotel. I left that job to start working for the Leukemia Society and I moved in with a friend from the hotel. Finally, I was starting to feel a little more comfortable. I was an adult living away from home with a job I liked. This felt like the script that I was meant to be following. This was what I was supposed to be doing. The checklist was activated again.

My job was to plan the fundraising events for the Leukemia Society, and that gave me the freedom to use some creativity. About one year in, I planned a Jell-O slide at Meramec College. People would get sponsors and then slide down into a giant above-ground pool filled with red Jell-O. It took a lot of coordination.

I asked a car wash to allow us to use its hot water to make Jell-O in 50 gallon barrels. Then I found someone to donate a refrigerated truck to haul it all. I got the college to donate the space for the event. We had to dump all of the Jell-O into the donated pool and arrange for the fire department to be stationed outside to hose people off. There is nothing like the sight of dozens of people coated in red Jell-O being hosed off by firefighters to make you enjoy your job.

It was fun work, and I liked being able to think outside the box, but I was already getting a little antsy. What happened to my clear script? What happened to my path to my future? I wasn't sure this was what I wanted to spend my life doing, either. Every time I got into a comfortable groove, I found myself holding my immediate experience up and imagining it into the future. It didn't have to just be the right job for now, it had to be the right job to fit my whole imagined future life. I couldn't see Jell-O slides for years to come. About a year and a half into this job, I got a phone call with an opportunity for adventure.

I never pass up a good adventure.

The phone rang in my office at the Leukemia Society. I was expecting something routine about an upcoming fundraiser, but the person on the other end wasn't calling about work. It was a woman I had known years before in youth group.

"What do you think about going to Israel?"

Sar-El, an Israeli program, was looking for volunteers to fill all the jobs that the soldiers on reserve duty had been called away from during the first Intifada. In Israel, everyone serves two years of compulsory military service straight out of high school. After that, they have two weeks a year of reserve service, but during the Intifada, they were taking everyone back to active duty. That's why Sar-El was looking to fill spots with volunteers in hospitals, on kibbutzim, and on army bases. These were the jobs the soldiers called to active duty were not performing.

"You'd be leaving in 10 days," she said.

I started thinking about what people would think about me if I just up and left this job. After all, I'd already jumped around from college to college, pieced together my degree, moved back in with my parents and back out, and was just starting to get my life together. I was working a job I was good at even though I was getting bored. I was an adult. I had responsibilities, but more than that, I had expectations to meet—expectations of my own making, even if they were formed by the voice of invisible, imagined spectators.

"Sorry," I said. "There's no way I could get away on such short notice." I hung up the phone and turned to go back to work.

Back to the work that was already feeling more like a routine than a challenge. A voice inside my head started asking questions. *Why not? You're 26. You aren't married. You don't have kids. You've already gotten what you can out of this job, and sure, it's been a good experience, but let's be honest, you're bored. You can totally go to Israel.*

That was crazy talk. My thoughts went back to: *What will people say? You've already been through a few jobs and dropped out of school. People are going to say you can't commit to anything.*

The first voice returned. *They aren't going to say that when you are going to volunteer to replace soldiers who are off risking their lives during fucking combat! You're not quitting your job to drink by the pool and eat bonbons. You're doing something that matters!*

Within five minutes I'd made my decision based on what I wanted and what felt right for me instead of what I "should" do according to other people. It was a choice that disrupted my already bumpy path to stability and the neat list of accomplishments I was still trying to tick off like clockwork, but I knew it was a good decision. It was one that was authentically me, something I would learn to appreciate much more as I got older. This was the right move.

There were just a few little hiccups to the plan. For instance, I didn't have a passport.

Never one to let obstacles stop me once I'd made a decision, I called my state senator and explained the situation. My passport was expedited. I got it four days later, less than a week before I would be leaving.

I had no interest in working in a hospital, and I had already been on a kibbutz when I went to Israel as a teen. That left the army base. I signed up.

I didn't know a soul. I spent the night before departure in the New York airport feeling proud of myself, excited about the adventure, and a little scared, to be honest.

The flight was full. I was on a 747 jumbo jet that had been chartered to take 700 volunteers, all going to take part in the same program. That wasn't enough space. This group filled half of a second jet as well. People of all ages: families, young singles like me—a diorama of people— filled the flight. It was amazing.

For Jews, there's something about arriving in Israel that makes you want to kiss the ground when you walk down the steps from the plane. During an awesome welcome ceremony on the tarmac, the Prime Minister spoke to our group. It was like having the President of the United States greet you when you got off the plane in New York. Incredible.

We were divided into groups, and each group was supposed to depart on a different charter bus heading for a different destination. They said everything in broken English, and it was dark. I had no idea which bus I was supposed to get on! Eventually, I just got on the one that I hoped was right. I'd end up in the right place, I reasoned.

On the bus, the leader was checking names, and called everyone's except mine. There was one name left over, and it was clearly not my name, but I wanted it to be, so I convinced myself that it could be my name... if you squinted... and mispronounced it... and it had maybe been misspelled. I raised my hand.

We drove north for a few hours until we arrived at an army tank maintenance base near the Sea of Galilee. It was two o'clock in the morning, and we were exhausted from traveling the past two days, but we still had to drag our suitcases up a steep hill in pitch darkness. We couldn't tell where we were or what was around us.

We were split up into rooms in an army barracks with two, three, or four people to a room. We had to wait until morning to see what the base looked like.

The next day, we were fit for uniforms. They were the same ones the soldiers wore, but ours had blue ribbons on the epaulettes to signal that we were volunteers. Our assigned uniform included pants, a shirt, boots, a beret, and a coat. It was a gigantic man's coat, and I loved it.

One of the women rooming with me was Robin from "DallasTexas." That's how she said it—not "Dallas," not "Texas," but "DallasTexas" like it was all one, slurred word. She was my age and had also come alone.

Our job was to do whatever menial tasks the army couldn't afford to use soldiers for. One day I cleaned the canisters that housed the missiles on the tanks. Another day I inventoried tank parts. One day I worked in the garden. It was something different every day. Our presence helped maintain some semblance of peace and routine.

I kind of had a "thing" going with the leader of our group. He was an Israeli man named Avigdor who was hot as hell! This added another level of excitement to my time there.

One day our group took a trip into town to blow off some steam and get some food. All of the volunteers had gone their separate ways, and Avigdor and I were walking around together. A little local boy came up to me and said something in Hebrew. Avigdor translated it for me after he walked away. "You're a very pretty soldier girl." He thought I was an Israeli soldier and not an American volunteer, and thought I was pretty! I loved that! I fit in! Aside from isolated moments, this is one of my earliest memories of feeling like I fit in to a community that I had worked hard to become a part of.

At the end of the trip, on the way to the airport, Avigdor and I were sharing a seat on the bus. "So," he said. I wondered what he was going to say to me. I had been sitting there sad, thinking about how I would never see him again. I wondered if he'd been thinking the same thoughts, wondering if we'd ever see each other again, wondering what I meant to him. "When they inventoried the uniforms, there was a coat missing," he said. "Was that you?"

"Nope, not me," I replied without missing a beat.

I still have that coat—I wore it two weeks ago. I don't know why, but I just love that coat. I run my fingers over the Hebrew words and wonder who else wore it, what other stories it has seen.

My trip to Israel brought so much richness to my life and was the catalyst for other life-changing experiences. This confirmed to me to never pass up any adventure or opportunity that feels right, no matter how far out of my comfort zone it takes me.

When I quit my job to go to Israel, I had arranged to work at Camp Sabra upon my return, but I had no idea what I was going to do after that. Here I was again, working without a script. I was proud of my adventures and happy to have taken them, but flying back toward home I started fretting about how far I had strayed from the plan. How was I going to get back on track? How was I going to start working on checking those items off my list to prove I had lived my life right? (Yes, here I was being pulled back in to the checklist of what was expected of me. It happened surreptitiously, without my even realizing I was about to swirl the drain again.)

Listen to this Reader, and listen good: growth is a process, two steps forward, one step back. That's okay. Sometimes those old thought patterns will just sneak up on you. Just keep taking the two steps forward and be kind to yourself throughout the process.

Robin and I had stayed in touch. "You should move to Dallas," she told me.

"Are you crazy?" I asked her.

"Come on!" she insisted. "You have nothing else to do!"

Who can argue with logic like that? Another adventure—another opportunity. It felt right.

I told her I would give it one month, but if I couldn't find a job by the end of the month, I would move back to St. Louis.

I flew to Dallas on a one-way ticket with a single suitcase of clothing.

When I got there, I stayed with Robin and found a job within a week, doing sales on a party ranch 30 miles north of Dallas. The next day I drove around and found an apartment I liked.

It was settled. Two days later I flew back to St. Louis, packed my stuff, and drove back to Dallas to move into my new apartment and begin my new life. Here was yet another chance for a fresh start. Maybe this time adulthood wouldn't slip out of my grasp. Maybe this time I was on my real path. Could I turn a job into a career, an apartment into a house, a cute guy into a husband? Maybe it was only a matter of time and a little hard work.

The truth is I was always waiting to start living my adult life. Of course, the fact is that I was already living it. This was all a journey to make it my own. How long would it take me to understand this? At what point would I realize that my adult life was happening whether I was acknowledging it or not? At what point would I grasp that the adult life that I wanted had to be on my own terms? The fact that life isn't what you want or imagine it to be doesn't mean it's not happening. I had to realize that the checklist wasn't the answer for me. But not yet. As I said, this was a process and I was right in the middle of it.

Here I was in DallasTexas, working on an honest-to-God ranch. It wasn't some little cutesy vacation spot dressed up to look like a ranch. It was the real deal. The ranch had an outbuilding that served as the kitchen, and there was a smoker outside that could hold 2,000 pounds of meat at once. It was bigger than a car! There was a professional-size, working rodeo and a live bull people could sit on and have their picture taken. Guests could book trail rides. They would travel out to a big clearing with a chuck wagon and have dinner by a campfire. The house band, The Texas Playboys (from Bob Wills & The Texas Playboys) were country music legends. It was a big deal that they played for us.

The ranch had 60-plus acres and an enormous barn that could hold parties of up to 4,000 people. A smaller building could accommodate parties of 20 to 150. We booked a lot of conferences for people who wanted to have a one-day event away from their Dallas and Fort Worth hotels. They'd come out for team building and entertainment. It was an awesome job for me. A part of me has always felt right at home being a cowgirl (and a hippie) even if the Jewish girl from suburban St. Louis in me wonders at the contradiction.

This job reignited that part of me that had loved being with the horses on my grandparents' farm when I was a girl. It was nice to wear jeans and cowboy boots every day and get to call them work clothes! To that point I had never been so comfortable in my own skin. I was in an environment I enjoyed and felt at home in, wearing clothes that suited my personality. I was surrounded by horses, music, and nature. I had taken risks to get there, but there I was and I was loving it.

Life was going pretty well.

One day I met a friend for lunch at Chuck E. Cheese so we could talk while her son played. I spent the entire lunch complaining because I had to go to work that night for a stupid Sheraton Christmas party! I'd have to drive over an hour and mess up a perfectly good Saturday night! I was supposed to schmooze all the Sheraton party planners and make connections so they would book parties with us in the future. It sounded like boring work, and I was not happy about it.

Night rolled around. I had made plans to meet up with Robin to listen to some music when the schmooze-fest was over. The Sheraton party was at the little barn, and a huge Mary Kay Christmas party was going on at the big barn that had more than 1,000 guests. I went into the small barn to find my boss, Derek, so he could introduce me to the people I needed to see.

Derek was a total ass—a kid, younger than I was. His dad let him run the place and he was an arrogant jerk about it.

When I arrived he was busy talking to two guys. One of them was Wes, a friend of Derek's from high school who had brought his coworker, Daniel. They worked together at the Lowes Anatole hotel in Dallas. Wes and Daniel were there because Derek had told them about the Mary Kay party with hundreds of women. They were both pretty cute guys. I remember asking myself which one I would choose.

My boss introduced us, and I stayed and talked to them for a while. Daniel was wearing khakis, topsiders, and a pink polo that was tucked in, but I could see that he had on a tie-dye shirt underneath. I invited them to meet up with Robin and me later that night—I still wasn't sure which one I would prefer as my date, if given the choice.

After I finished working at the meet and greet, I met Robin, and the guys joined us. Wes and Robin were on one side of the table and Daniel and I were on the other.

I picked Daniel. Maybe it was the tie-dye shirt. We got married a year later.

I'd spent so much time worrying about my path through adulthood, about getting it right, and now it was clear to me that the Universe already had a plan. But it was a plan that I needed to take an active role in through the choices I made. If I hadn't said yes to that random phone call inviting me to go to Israel on a whim, I wouldn't have met Robin. If I hadn't met Robin, I wouldn't have packed up my whole life and moved to DallasTexas. And if I hadn't done that, I never would have met Daniel.

Daniel didn't live in Dallas. He was a student at the Culinary Institute of America, where he was also undertaking a career change. He was on a six-month externship from the program. Once he finished, he had nine months of school left in New York.

When we started dating I would stay at his hotel some nights and go straight from there to work. I felt like I was doing the walk of shame every morning as I walked past the doormen.

Daniel's externship was half way over when we met. By the time he was getting ready to go back to New York, we knew we were getting married. I tried to keep working at the ranch while flying to visit him, but that schedule was grueling. I couldn't keep it up! Traveling to and from upstate New York took up two whole days, so anything shorter than a five-day trip was a waste of time. You can only ask for so much time off after having been on the job for only a few months.

I knew I wanted to live in St. Louis after we got married, so I went ahead and moved back. I rented a house for us to live in while waiting for Daniel to graduate. All in all, I was in Dallas for six months. Robin couldn't believe that she'd spent her whole life there and hadn't met someone special yet, and I had found my someone special after a couple of months!

Even though we knew marriage was in our future, we weren't officially engaged yet. He was still in school, but he was planning to visit St. Louis for the Fourth of July weekend. We were going to a house at the Lake of the Ozarks with my family, and Daniel had made dinner reservations for just the two of us at a really nice restaurant overlooking the lake. I was convinced that he would propose there. It would be the perfect spot!

Before we headed to the lake, we decided to take part in the Fourth of July festivities on the St. Louis riverfront. We went to see the Neville Brothers concert under the Arch. I was standing on a picnic table so I could see the band, and Daniel was standing on the ground next to me. We were surrounded by people who knew us, including my sister and several friends.

We'd been talking about a Grateful Dead show in Wisconsin the following weekend, and Daniel had mentioned that he wanted to go. I knew it would cut into our brief time together before he had to go back to school, and I didn't want him to leave.

He turned to me and said, "I have something to ask you." *Shit!* I thought. *He's going to ask me to go to that damned concert. How can I say no without looking like a bitch in front of him and all of these people?*

"Will you marry me?"

He had caught me totally off guard. I knew it was coming because I had worked with the jeweler on the ring setting, but it still took me completely by surprise. And he'd been carrying around a large diamond in his pocket during Fair Saint Louis! I was trembling. It turned out everyone around us knew he was going to ask me that night, so they were all waiting for my response.

"Yes!"

He had to help me off the table because I was shaking so hard, and then he said, "I didn't have to get down on one knee because you were already above me." We left in the middle of the concert.

I was so happy I wanted to call everyone I knew.

As we walked away from the Arch, arms around one another, we heard the fireworks going off behind us. It was picture perfect, and I couldn't have been happier.

Buckle Up, It's Going to be a Bumpy Ride

Things were moving right along. I had married the man of my dreams—and now our new family was already expanding. I got pregnant on our honeymoon!

I was following the footsteps of my parents, finally moving forward on the path I was supposed to be walking (right?). After some false starts and detours, my winding, overgrown path was starting to look like a paved straightaway. You've always got to watch for those speed bumps, though.

I didn't know if I was having a girl or a boy. I had been part of a study at Washington University to explore the benefits of ultrasounds, and I was randomly assigned to the control group. That meant I didn't have any ultrasounds unless they were medically necessary. Because of that, it wasn't until I had an internal exam the week leading up to my due date that I found out my baby was breach. The doctor scheduled a C-section for the next week.

This wasn't the plan. But ironically, it allowed me to plan and schedule everything for an event that is normally spontaneous. I had the day and time that my baby was going to be born. I called my Lamaze coach to cancel the rest of the sessions because obviously those had been a waste of time. I was working as the assistant to the director of Camp Sabra, so I needed to get my position covered. It had been a busy day. There was so much to focus on to be ready!

Finally, around 10 o'clock, Daniel and I climbed into bed. I was in bed for maybe 30 seconds when I heard the pop. It hit me. *Oh my God. I think my water just broke.* I ran to the bathroom so fast that I don't think the bed even got wet.

I called my doctor, who told me to head to the hospital right away.

"Okay. Can I just jump in the shower and shave my legs?" I asked.

"Absolutely not!" she responded. The cord could possibly prolapse and drop into the birth canal since my waters had broken. I needed to get to the hospital as soon as possible. I hadn't even packed a bag yet. We hadn't picked a name for the baby. On the way down to the hospital, we were still throwing names back and forth.

In the car I started having contractions. By the time I got to my room, the contractions were bad—at least for a person with a pretty low pain threshold. When we got there, the only anesthesiologist on staff that late at night was in surgery. I was in full-blown labor, punching Daniel in the stomach rhythmically with the rise of each increasingly painful knot tying itself across my abdomen. Worst of all, I knew all this pain was for nothing because I was going to end up with a C-section anyway!

My nurse was a big, blonde, soft, round woman who had me sit on the edge of the bed when they *finally* came in to do the epidural.

"Just lay your head right here, honey," she said as she patted her chest. She was like a huge pillow, and I sank into her. I didn't have any energy left to worry about whether it was appropriate to sink my head into this woman's breasts. All I could think about was how soothing it was. The epidural went off without a hitch, and I lay back down.

"How was that contraction?" the doctor asked.

"What contraction?" I asked. Now that the drugs were working, I was back in the game.

As the anesthesiologist walked out the door, I called after him. "What's your name? I'm naming this baby after you! Thank you, thank you, thank you!" Of course, I didn't name my daughter after him, but I sure meant it in that moment.

My doctor met me in the surgical suite. The mood was light and calm. Dr. F. was chipper as always, but I was concerned about her. It was after midnight, and she was seven months pregnant herself! Throughout the surgery I would periodically check on her. "Hey, how you doing? You okay?" She kept assuring me she was fine, and soon she introduced us to our first daughter who, from the beginning, has been the most caring, giving person I have ever known.

Here I was, living happily ever after.

There is a false belief that if we check all the boxes and follow the program we will have a happy, perfect life without challenges or tragedies.

The idea that checked boxes will protect us from bad things is just a fantasy. It is not a formula for avoiding the hard times life has in store for us.

So, if in real life the good and the bad are going to happen no matter what, we need to stop worrying about checking the boxes and live as authentically as we can. Dear Readers, live for happiness, not for checking things off the list!

Myth Buster: if you can make your life look perfect then it will be.

When my daughter was almost two years old, I saw a raised red spot on my arm. I headed to the dermatologist for a biopsy and a lot of blood work, but they couldn't find a vein! Drawing my blood has always been a problem for me, but this time was the worst. The doctor sent me to the hospital for the blood work. I'd already been poked eight times. The phlebotomist at the hospital couldn't get a vein either, so she sent me back to the doctor's office. Finally, the doctor came in and tried to find a vein. Success! Both of my arms and hands were covered in bruises and bandages, but the blood finally flowed.

The first of the biopsy results came back inconclusive. The doctor thought I might have Lyme disease, but couldn't be sure without running more tests. She put me on medicine to treat Lyme while we waited two weeks for the results to come back. In the meantime, she was sure about two things: I had subacute cutaneous lupus (or so she said at the time) and sarcoidosis.

Sarcoidosis was big, scary news. I had to tell my family, and I wanted to let my grandparents know right away. I called and told them that I was coming over. The medicine I was on for Lyme disease made me nauseous. That particular day it was so bad that I had to pull over on the way to their house to puke by the side of the highway. Then I got back in my car and continued on.

As soon as my grandparents opened the door, I had to throw up again! I rushed past them, gagging all the way to the bathroom.

Of course, my grandparents assumed I was pregnant even though I never threw up during my first pregnancy. Now I had to break it to them that not only was I not pregnant, but I had been diagnosed with a whole gamut of diseases.

A week later, I found out I didn't have Lyme disease after all, so that awesome medication was for nothing!

The doctor said subacute cutaneous lupus was the official explanation for the painful and ugly reaction my skin had to concentrated exposure to the sun. It is different from systemic lupus. However, sarcoidosis is a systemic disease where granulomas form in your body. They can form anywhere! In addition to finding the one on my skin, my granulomas found a comfy home in my lungs and eventually my lymph system.

I was also told that I was Rh positive. This is a blood type issue that could complicate any future pregnancies by crossing into the placenta. Eventually, the subacute cutaneous lupus diagnosis was changed to polymorphous light eruption (PMLE), another autoimmune issue caused by the sun. Imagine heat rash or sun poisoning on steroids. That is what it looks like on me, and the pain and itching make me crazy—scratch-the-skin-off-my-body crazy. For light episodes I use a steroid cream, but more severe episodes require oral steroids. It's not a great condition for someone who loves being outdoors and was already so body conscious.

The following year, I started seeing a rash on my outer thighs. It hurt to touch, and then it turned black. My dermatologist was completely stumped. I spent years trying creams and other topical treatments until she finally, out of frustration, sent me to "grand rounds" at the hospital.

Assuming you've never had the joy of being a living lab specimen, let me tell you a little about grand rounds. Forty doctors march past you, staring at you like a bug in a jar, taking notes and tilting their heads with curiosity. Then they break into little groups and talk about you like you're not sitting right in front of them. Occasionally they'll glance back at you suspiciously, this specimen that's giving them so much trouble.

The gaggle of doctors stuck their heads together, murmured decisively to one another, and determined I had perniosis. My dermatologist, one of the best in St. Louis, hadn't thought of that diagnosis because it's thought to be biologically impossible for one person to have both PMLE and perniosis. They're histological opposites. But that's me! I'm a woman who can have it all!

PMLE flares in the heat and sun, and perniosis flares in the wet and cold. One winter we were taking a cruise. My annual perniosis flare-up was in full swing, and I got PMLE while we were cruising. I had two diseases that were supposed to be impossible to have in the same body *at the same time. Are you fucking kidding me with this?*

On top of all of that, I was still dealing with the sarcoidosis, where the granulomas had filled the home they had made in my lungs with little baby granulomas and distant relatives. It was a real party in there! My oxygen saturation rate went to a low of 74 percent, which is bad, really bad. As my doctors discussed the options, I was told that the only treatment was high-dose steroids. I didn't want to take them because steroids can really mess up your body. I didn't want to gain all the weight and deal with the other side effects of steroids, so instead I made a different choice. I did nothing. Yes, doing nothing is a choice.

My uncle, a doctor, brought me in for a "come to Jesus" meeting.

"You need to pick a doctor, and you need to start treatment now," he told me. "You should be walking around with an oxygen tank."

Things weren't going to get better by ignoring them, and it was time that I faced it. I was always tired from lack of oxygen and couldn't even run around and play with my daughter.

The steroids were horrific. My initial dose was too strong and ate a hole in my stomach (this is probably not exactly the way the doctor would describe it). I ended up in the hospital to get all of the steroids out of my system and then start the entire process over at a lower, but still high, dosage.

The steroids made me moody. I was snapping at people and uncomfortable about my appearance. I gained a lot of weight because the steroids made me hungry all the time, and my cheeks became cushingoid. I was unrecognizable to myself. It seemed as if my face was

beth koritz

twice its normal size. I looked like a chipmunk with acne (another gift of steroids).

I couldn't emotionally handle even the most routine of setbacks. For instance, I was remodeling a bathroom in the house, and when the contractor said he was finished, I went in to look at it. Everything looked great... except the walls. He had used only one coat of paint, which I could see through. When I told him the walls needed a second coat, something that should have been a simple task and was an obvious need, he told me that he put only one coat of paint in the bid and would charge me to do more. I told him that was ridiculous because the room wasn't done until the paint was done.

He started arguing with me about it. It was a very small space. We are talking about an hour of his time and half a gallon of paint. It was so absurd and so frustrating to be arguing over this that I started crying. It was a ridiculous overreaction on my part, but I had no control over it. I walked out and retreated to the basement.

For all the trouble they caused, the steroids worked the way they were supposed to work, and I went into remission, but let me tell you, those pills took their toll. I gained 30 pounds and had hot flashes like I was going through menopause. I could only wear loose-fitting shoes because of my swollen feet, and I had acne worse than I did when I was 15. I didn't recognize myself, and I hated even walking by a mirror.

I stopped going out. It was embarrassing. I was turning 30 during that year, and Daniel wanted to throw me a party. I told him over and over again that I didn't want one. I was not comfortable being seen by anybody. But he did it anyway.

I had a feeling he was up to something. One night we came home from an early dinner, and as we pulled into the driveway at the back of the house, I could see lots of people inside through the windows. He had planned a surprise party! All I wanted to do was crawl under a rock and disappear, but I had to smile and pretend I was having a good time. I was miserable!

It took six more months to wean me off the steroids. The side effects started to subside as the dosage got lower. My skin cleared up and my cheeks de-puffed, but some of the weight held on.

The following year I became pregnant with my second daughter. Because of the Rh antibody identified during my diagnoses, I was marked as a high-risk pregnancy from the very beginning. I had so many ultrasounds in that pregnancy it made up for the lack of them in the first one. Early on we found out that this baby was also breach.

They told me it was almost unheard of to have two breach pregnancies without some kind of physical abnormality. Almost unheard of until they met me! *If it can happen, it will happen to me!* That was my motto at the time.

My doctor was hopeful that the baby would move, but month after month she was in the same position. With one week of the pregnancy to go, the doctor suggested version to try to avoid a second C-section. Version is when the doctor tries to manually turn the baby into a different position by kneading your belly like a ball of dough. My baby had been comfortably lounging in the same spot for five months! I tried to tell him it wasn't going to work. I knew she wasn't going to budge from that position.

"I have an 85 percent success rate," the doctor bragged.

"Well, get ready for it to be lower," I quipped.

I went to the hospital for the version, and the doctor was pushing and rolling my belly. Nothing happened. "I'll be right back," he said. When he returned, he brought in another doctor he'd grabbed from the hallway. The two of them were lumbering over me like they were peering under the hood of a smoking car they were determined to fix. These two men pushed on my belly as hard as they could. It hurt like hell! They went on like that for several minutes, four huge hands digging into my tender, pregnant belly. This was yet more pain I had to go through for absolutely no reason, and I rolled my eyes between grimaces because I knew from the beginning that it wasn't going to work.

They finally admitted defeat and told me to go home and get some rest. That was on Friday. The following Monday, my regular OB called and told me my amniotic fluid was low. They needed to do a C-section right away.

The original C-section date had been scheduled in advance, so I thought I could avoid the last-minute scrambling of my first delivery, but here I was again. I was at a close friend's house with my daughter for a children's birthday party. I spent the rest of the afternoon on her phone getting everything lined up. The C-section would be the next morning.

I comforted myself with the fact that at least this time I wouldn't have to experience contractions first. I could just start with an epidural from the beginning. We arrived at 7 a.m., and I was taken into the operating room to get prepped. Then they were ready to insert the epidural, and the damned thing wouldn't go in. They tried and tried, but they couldn't get the needle in the epidural space.

They decided to call someone else to try. In the meantime they had me laid out with my legs spread, exposed for all the world to see.

"Could you please cover me?" I asked. They'd just been standing over me chatting like I didn't exist. It was strange, but at this moment I felt a small sense of pride for standing up for myself and asking those in authority for what I needed to be comfortable.

Finally, the other anesthesiologist arrived, and he came up behind me and stabbed me in the back with the needle. It was like he was spear fishing. I screamed. By the time I turned around to look at him, he was gone. I never even saw his face.

The medical team began poking me in the stomach to test to make sure I was completely numb, but I wasn't. I had a window of pain about the size of a softball in the center of my belly.

They kept increasing the epidural medication, but the window wouldn't close. Finally, they got it high enough to work properly. In the meantime, Daniel had been waiting in the hallway for more than 40 minutes, and he was freaking out because no one had told him what was going on.

It was finally all set. The epidural was working. Daniel was in the room. My second daughter was born during an annular eclipse, when the moon passes in front of the sun but doesn't completely obscure it, so a halo of light appears around the moon. This was a perfect time for her to enter the world. She is always a ray of light, brightening the darkest of times.

Welcome to the world, baby!

Warning: Road Might Flood

Two years later, when my youngest daughter was in preschool, I started to have sharp pains in my stomach. As I mentioned, I have a pretty low pain tolerance, so I went to the doctor right away.

"Eat some yogurt," she said. "You should feel better soon."

A few days went by and I wasn't getting better. In fact, I was feeling even worse. By this point I was writhing in bed at night. I couldn't sleep. I just moaned and groaned. A whole week went by this way.

On the Wednesday before Memorial Day weekend, a holiday that would continue being a frequent harbinger of bad news for me, I was moaning in bed again and Daniel said: "For God's sake! You're keeping me up all night. Either go to the emergency room or quit complaining because I can't sleep with you like this!"

That day, two friends came over to see the house that we had just finished building. I was really proud of it because we had sourced everything ourselves. We had brought in unique spiral wood columns from Santa Fe and had many features custom made.

This home truly reflected my personality. It couldn't have been more different from the typical homes being built in St. Louis at the time. I was giving my friends the grand tour, and kept doubling over in pain. At one point I almost collapsed to the ground.

"This is ridiculous," my friend said. "You need to go to a doctor!" I told her I couldn't because I had to get Dallas from preschool. "I'll get her!"

My doctor told me to come in right away. I got to the waiting room and no one was there. As I sat with tears running down my face, the doctor came out. She said she'd been waiting for me. She pushed on my belly, and I screamed. "You need to get to the ER," she said. "*Now!*"

I drove myself to the hospital and called my mom and Daniel on my clunky cell phone. When I got to the hospital, I didn't know what to do. I was thinking I couldn't pull into the ER drive because there was no one to move my car. (Seriously, who thinks like that when they are crying in pain?) I parked in the garage and walked, doubled over and wincing with each step. The ER was on the other end of the hospital. I hunched over and pushed my fists into my gut, willing myself to make it all the way without collapsing.

My doctor had called ahead, so I was in surgery to have my appendix removed before Daniel even got there.

Normally, an appendectomy can be done laparoscopically, but I had a mass on my appendix, so the surgeon had to do a full incision across my belly. With this and the scars from my two C-sections, my midsection was becoming quite the elaborate road map.

I was in the hospital for a full week because I started running a fever and couldn't be released. Daniel and I missed our Memorial Day trip to Vancouver Island, which was supposed to have been our anniversary celebration. My Memorial Day weekends were beginning to have a theme.

During this time when things were beginning to unravel, my carefully constructed road was starting to flood. I have become a firm believer that the Universe has a plan. When things go awry, I reason that the Universe is subtly (or sometimes not-so-subtly) pushing me into self-correction, getting me back on the right path.

Sometimes, though, we're lucky enough to land on a track where everything seems to fall into place. There's no nudging us back into place necessary. Everything just *works*.

At first, it looked like the Universe had put me on the dream track with the phone call that led to my going to Israel and thus meeting Daniel. Leading up to our marriage, Daniel and I had a great, active life, with enough excitement to keep me interested and satisfied. He was always whisking me off to wonderful restaurants or to listen to fun music. I imagined a life with him full of exhilaration and adventure.

But it was easy to be exhilarated in those early days of courtship. By the time we were both living in St. Louis, planning the wedding consumed most of our time. We knew that we didn't want to wait too long to start a family. I figured it would take a few months to get pregnant, so I stopped taking my birth control pills the week of the wedding. Boy, was I wrong about the timing.

We went from the exciting getting-to-know-you phase to the married-and-pregnant phase with no transition time. What was once all about impulsive dinners out and travel to fun places became all about finding a house and settling down. We had a baby on the way, and we needed stability!

Daniel had a job as a chef. He worked a lot of hours and wasn't his own boss. It was frustrating for him to have full responsibility of the kitchen but not the business. The failures were all his but the successes belonged to someone else. It was clear that the risks and stresses of such a schedule needed to be balanced out by the rewards of ownership.

The night we met, we had talked about owning a restaurant together and having our kids play in the back room. It would be a family place where the kids could grow up and the two of us would share the burden of work together. We'd be partners in the business and in the home—share and share alike.

From the outside looking in, we had the perfect marriage. We never fought. We got along great and seemed to have our plans in sync. He's the never-met-a-stranger kind of guy; he's a good person.

When our oldest daughter, Dylan, was two, we bought a restaurant of our own—a Jewish deli. It was the start of fulfilling our dreams. I was lengthening the path of this life that I'd been set on. The deli was open from 7 a.m. to 3 p.m. Tuesday through Sunday. I was already busy with a toddler when we bought the place and gave birth to our second daughter shortly after. Daniel was up and out the door by 5:30 every morning, and he wouldn't come home until 6 in the evening, exhausted.

I tried to make our dream a reality. I put Dallas in daycare, and Dylan in preschool. I would work the lunch rush and handle the business side of the restaurant: balancing the books, paying the bills, etc. We had a partner who had also graduated from the Culinary Institute, but somehow having someone take on half the responsibility had no impact on Daniel's availability at home. The restaurant started to get all of him. He didn't have anything left to give when he got home.

As a Jewish deli, naturally our biggest days of the year were catering for the Jewish holidays. That meant that our own family's holidays were spent with Daniel working 36 hours straight. Even if he did manage to sneak away to show up at any events, he wasn't really there. I was doing my part and running the business end of the restaurant, but I was also running all of our home and family.

At the same time, we were building our dream house together. I was making every architectural and design choice on my own. It became a full-time job for me. I was easily putting in 40 hours a week building the house, ordering materials, and bringing in the décor from New Mexico and Mexico. It was a dream, but it was mostly my dream. Daniel was happy to go along.

I began feeling like a single parent. He was great with the kids when he was around, but he wasn't around often. He worked all weekend every weekend, with Monday his only day off. It didn't feel like a partnership, and it certainly didn't feel like what we had planned.

I was a real hippie mom. I was cooking my own baby food, pureeing the vegetables, and grinding organic turkey. I was always scrambling to make our house a home and make sure our children felt loved and cared for. On top of that, I was moving back and forth between disease and recovery, constantly trying to find my balance. It was exhausting, and I felt like I was doing it all alone.

We were having a party in the backyard for Dallas's fourth birthday. It was a Saturday, and I had to get "no parking" signs from the city to block off one side of the street. I had all these people—including lots of kids!—coming to my house, and I was out in the May sun pounding tomato stakes into the ground. The party was in three hours, and I realized I had done everything myself. All the planning, all the cleaning, all the preparation, all the tomato staking: it was all me. Standing in the sun I had an overwhelming visceral experience of how alone I was.

Daniel came home from the restaurant and sauntered into the party late, still wearing his chef pants and work shirt, as he moved among the patio full of people. He put on a clown nose and made some jokes. There he was: the life of the party. All the kids thought he was so cute and funny. An hour and a half later, the party was over and he was back at work. I was left with the entire mess to clean up on my own.

I resented having to be everything while he got to focus on one thing. It was impossible to feel like I was doing anything right when I was pulled in so many different directions, and Daniel didn't seem to notice the imbalance.

Maybe someone learning all this would think that I had all the control over our lives: that I was calling the shots. Maybe I did. When it came to the marriage, I ran it. When it came to the house, I ran it. I made all the decisions. I *was* the marriage, but that's not what a marriage is supposed to be. I didn't *want* to have to be in control. I wanted to have a partner.

At that time I was feeling especially vulnerable to the twists and turns of fate and that I had very little control over much of my life. Those illnesses happened *to* me. Even my sometimes-wayward path through jobs and college had seemed like a stream where I was pulled along, waiting to find the place to take hold and gain control over my own life.

But that wasn't the case with my marriage. I felt like I had some control there. I had decided to get married. I had decided to become a mother. I had decided to build a house and a business and a family with a man I loved. It was a way of taking over the narrative, of making sure that my story was what I wanted it to be.

It was like a sandcastle we had built together, and it was beautiful: big, strong, and impressive to behold. We had the kids, the house, the business, the love. We had it all. But sandcastles don't stay up by themselves. Waves and wind hit them. They erode from all sides. They take constant, vigilant work to maintain, and Daniel had helped me build our sandcastle and then lost focus on everything but work.

The waves kept washing off the front of our sandcastle, so I just kept scrambling to rebuild it in the back. Over time, I realized that none of the original castle was left. Nothing that Daniel had helped me build remained. It wasn't our castle anymore; it was mine. I was doing all the building myself, and if I was going to do all the work, I figured I might as well build it the way *I* want it.

My castle had gotten mighty fucking lonely.

All the things that tethered me to Daniel started to erode like that sand. I was left with routine, habits—the motions of a relationship without the passion behind them. We lost the day-to-day interactions. We no longer had conversations about what we'd have for dinner; we no longer snuck hugs over our children's heads, or hands held on walks. All those things had eroded away, too.

At that point, there was nothing left to save. Once the emotional connection eroded, the physical one wasn't far behind. It was a chicken-and-egg question. Were we not being physical because we didn't have an emotional connection or were we not having an emotional connection because we stopped having a physical one? Ultimately, it didn't matter. The foundation was gone.

In situations like this, people start to draw lines in the sand. How long can we expect to do it all on our own? Until the kids are older? Until they graduate high school? College? Until the house is paid off? Until you meet someone else? Until... until... until...

Merge Ahead

I believe that everything happens for a reason. It's a cliché, sure, but that doesn't mean it's untrue. It's funny how I need to remind myself of this during unpleasant times. If I apply for a job I really like and don't get it, then I'll console myself by remembering that everything happens for a reason. If I apply for the same job and *do* get it, well, the reason is clear: it was the right job for me at the time! It's a lot easier to excuse the outcomes as fate when they're outcomes we don't want. When we get the outcomes we desire, of course, we're happy to take the credit!

Sometimes saying that everything happens for a reason can verge into the territory of giving up responsibility for our own lives. If I put the blame on some external force (or higher power), then I can just sit back and let life happen to me. However, this is just an excuse to avoid the challenging work of being present and taking action in our lives. That's why I've always taken issue with the phrase "let go and let God." I understand that it can just mean, "have faith," but it has to mean having faith in myself also—that *I'll* do the right thing and make the right choices and courageously take action. I do not believe I can just depend on some higher power to make sure everything happens the way it is supposed to without playing an active role in it. I am the one who takes responsibility for what happens in my life.

Every outcome has a reason, but that doesn't mean that our outcomes are chosen for us. We are not on a predetermined path, being guided along without having any say in where we go. It simply means that what is happening around us (or, as we often perceive it at the time, what is happening *to* us) is sending us messages about what choices we should have made or will make in the future. More often than not, the reason unpleasant or difficult things happen in our lives is to provide us with a path of self-correction, a gentle (or not-so-gentle) nudge to get on better paths.

The connections between the lesson learned and our future choices aren't always clear in the moment. It might not even be a lesson for the person we are today. It may be for our future selves, or our past selves.

We have lessons to learn—some small, some huge. The Universe gives us opportunity after opportunity to learn these lessons. If we don't, we're going to keep getting more opportunities. If your lesson is to use your voice and not let people push you around, the Universe is constantly going to give you another experience where someone *is* pushing you around. As soon as you've learned that lesson and find your voice and stand up for yourself, you're going to notice that you don't need to do it nearly as often.

I believe that our souls go through many journeys over the course of time, so you may be learning lessons today for future or past lifetimes. The journey is long, and what looks like a mountain in the road at the moment may be merely a pebble that fades to invisibility in the full scope of your being.

Often, though, our lessons are more tangible than that. If you think really hard, I bet you can remember events that felt unfair, unfathomable, and unbearable in the past that you now don't even consider on a regular basis. If you really examine them now, through your current eyes and with the benefit of time passed and life lived, you can probably identify the *why*. Think about the times those experiences changed your actions. Were there challenging times in the past that existed to make sure you acted, thought, or felt differently later?

When bad things happen (and they *will* happen), it is our challenge to find the reasons, possibly lessons, in them and the courage to be strong and resilient.

My lesson with being diagnosed with GBS, a situation that certainly was not "good," was a forced opportunity to focus on the positives in my life (although I could have easily gone the other way into negative thinking). I created an entirely new mindset for myself. Before that diagnosis, I had been speeding through life like I was on an interstate, ticking off the boxes I thought made a life worth living. Marriage? Check. Kids? Check. Career? Check. House? Check. But was I passing important landmarks that I should have been paying attention to? Was this even the right road for me?

I was spending so much time making sure I was doing things right that I didn't stop to think if they were right for me. The authentic me was struggling to be free. I don't regret the choices I made. I have wonderful children I love more than anything. I had a relationship that had many wonderful aspects to it. *Clearly this road often merged with the one that was my authentic path many times.*

From the moment I woke up paralyzed in that hospital bed, I realized that I had to reprioritize my life. I needed to focus on the positive, make a life full of great memories for my children, and take advantage of every positive opportunity that came my way.

I am here in this life to live and grow and connect spiritually to the world around me, the people who are important in my life, and with myself.

 Tools to Help You Focus on the Road

Once I was firm in my positive attitude and embraced the thought that my authentic self didn't have to fit into anybody else's expectations, finding my path that this lesson was guiding me toward became a lot easier. I was no longer eager to stay in my comfort zone, fighting the uncomfortable lessons that were pushing and prodding me. Instead, I was able to move fluidly and purposefully toward a deeper understanding. I didn't have all the answers, but I knew I was finally asking the right questions.

How did I cultivate a positive attitude? I asked myself these questions:

- Am I unhappy more than I'm happy?
- Do I find myself complaining a lot?
- What can I control?
- What actions can I take?

- Do I find myself ending my day thinking there was good in it? Was there joy?
- If I ask myself when I last smiled or laughed, can I answer? Was it longer ago than the sun rising this morning?

I had to answer those questions honestly and take responsibility for those outcomes. In the future, what can I do differently? Which emotions or actions do I need to repeat, and which ones do I need to delete? I shifted my focus from one of lack to one of gratitude and abundance. I thought about all the wonderful things in my life. When I found myself focusing on negative things, I thought about how I could change them. What actions did I need to take? I made lists of what brought me joy and committed to doing at least one of those things every single day. I focused on what I wanted my future to look like.

The possibilities were limitless. If I imagined what my fantasy life would look like with no concern of being judged or of money, what would that be? Then I thought about how I could choose some of the details from that fantasy and integrate them in to the life I had. I also had to take actions to move away from what and who I identified as having a negative impact on my life. My journey was about small steps and giant leaps. I still had a lifetime ahead of me to make it all happen. While part of being positive is taking action, it is also about being patient and kind to ourselves. This is the path to attaining what we perceive to be unattainable.

Look. We all have our moments. I can't pretend to you that I wake up like Susie Sunshine every morning with a smile plastered across my face no matter what the day has in store. I can't say that I never fall into a pity party or a bitch fest. I do. We all do.

But when this place of negativity and feeling sorry for ourselves becomes our daily norm, we lose perspective; we lose the ability to see the bigger picture.

If every morning you wake up and complain to your partner about your situation (the housekeeping, the bills, the kids' behavior, whatever it is that keeps you drained all day), then that script becomes rote. You end up saying your lines without even thinking through what they mean. There are all kinds of social media memes and supposed-to-be-funny jokes about having a "case of the Mondays" to demonstrate how awful we feel about our work lives. If we carry that language through our conversations with our co-workers and our daily interactions in our workspace, then misery on Monday becomes not a reaction to reality but an expectation to uphold.

Keep Looking Forward

If you say "Bad things always happen to me" or "I'll never be able to do this," you may create a self-fulfilling prophesy. This is where I was during what felt like a never-ending onslaught of health issues. I saw myself as having a target on my back, someone who was the victim of circumstances beyond her control, and my internal monologue was full of phrases that took the responsibility off of me and placed them onto the world at large.

In my therapy practice, I'm always challenging my clients to be aware of their language and reminding them to choose their words carefully. Language does not just name what is already happening. It also creates an energy in our consciousness that is sent out into the Universe. Our words can change our experiences.

This applies not just to day-to-day frustrations but also to larger-than-life events that sucker punch us and leave us gasping for air. Getting fired, going through a breakup, ending a friendship, having a house foreclosed on, wrecking a car: these are the moments where we are most likely to see the deck stacked against us, to perceive the world as out to get us and to think that nothing we do is going to matter anyway.

We are human. Sometimes we can't help but go to that place where we're feeling sorry for ourselves. Sometimes the sting of the rejection or the pain of the loss is so severe that we need to first retreat and heal before we can take the next step. Boldly practice self-compassion. Give yourself time to experience those feelings and process them. Name them. *This is grief. This is anger. This is shame.* But don't fall into the trap of getting stuck there. These things are real, but they are not permanent. These feelings are strong, but they are not you.

Take a Break

For me, I give myself the day. If things are going particularly awry, I call the day early. I go to bed. *It's 7:30, and I'm calling it. Tomorrow when I wake up, it's a fresh new day with a new outlook.* My girls have learned this lesson from me. "Shitty day, Mom. I'm calling it early, just like you taught me."

The next day, I put intention into living in gratitude. What I mean is that I look at the world around me and take stock. I force myself out of the pinhole perspective of pity and anger, emotions that narrow my point of view until I lose sight of everything else. Sometimes it can be hard to push them away, to broaden the edges around me. That's not a reason to stop trying.

The band The Bottle Rockets has a song with the lyric "I'm a wheel no matter what shape I'm in—always rolling forward." That line really resonates with me.

Whether I am paralyzed in a hospital bed, stuck flat on my back in a brace, rocked because of a bankruptcy, or making my dreams come true, I'm always striving to stay positive, moving forward, and rolling on. That doesn't mean I don't have dark days or moments. It just means that I work hard to acknowledge my dark feelings, figure out the why of it, determine what I can do about it, and do it! I don't let myself stay in that dark place. I examine what negative thinking got me there in order to turn it around. We might get "bent out of shape," but as long as we remain wheels, we'll be able to roll with it.

Appreciate the Journey

I ask my clients to keep a gratitude journal. You don't have to be a writer. This isn't poetry or the great American novel. This is a bullet point list. List five things you are grateful for each day. It can be simple.

- The sun is shining.
- I had the best hamburger for dinner.
- I had a great phone call with my mom.
- A rebate check came in the mail.
- I crossed two things off my To Do list.

Sometimes people get hung up on finding big things to be grateful for, and they miss all the everyday things that are going on around them. Not every day is going to come with a promotion or a party filled with your best friends, and if every day did come with those things, we'd stop appreciating them anyway. Every day, though, brings things that should make us thankful.

Sometimes people will tell me they can't find anything. They will say that nothing about their day has been worth celebrating. I'll push back. "Did you get here without having an accident? Did you get to kiss your husband goodbye this morning? Is the weather nice?"

Another way to make gratitude evident in your life is to be intentional about doing random acts of kindness. These don't have to be big. You don't have to spend hours volunteering or give up all your worldly possessions (though we learn from people who have done those things that gratitude grows when we turn outward). It can be as simple as telling the cashier at the grocery store to have a good day. You can tell a stranger that you really like her jacket—give her something to smile about. These tiny acts of kindness add up. They are the seeds of gratitude sown, and the more you scatter them around you, the more your daily journey will be filled with appreciation.

When you make someone else's day brighter, you can't help but feel a little bit better about your own. I have one client who straightens and organizes the grocery carts in the parking lot. He once had that job, and he wants to do a random act of kindness for the person doing it now.

Get Back On The Road

I said earlier that I give myself a day, but a day isn't always enough. If you didn't get into the school of your choice, maybe you need a week. If you're still floating in your sense of despair two weeks later, though, it's time to work at moving on. Don't let what you perceive as failure grow bigger than it has any right to be. Remember that while it's initially disappointing, there's a reason you won't be going there. Don't give it too much power over you and your future. Remember: identify your feelings, validate them, and examine what is in your control to change the situation.

Losses Along the Way

Some traumas are too big for a timeline. If you've lost a loved one, for example, allow yourself time. Grief is a process, and it can be a lengthy one. Be aware over time if you don't feel like you're progressing through the stages, and seek professional help.

The first thing to do when processing your feelings is identify them. *This is sadness.* There is no timetable for sadness. *This is blame.* Well, that has an expiration date. *This is self-pity.* That has the life expectancy of a mayfly. Let it go. Refocus on gratitude. You will remain sad about the loss of a loved one forever. You might carry some of that pain and loss around with you for the rest of your life. You might never get completely over that grief. But the anger, the blame, and the self-pity can be dealt with. Don't let those feelings restrict your life for too long. Define what "healed" looks like to you. I often have clients say, "When I am healed...." or, "When I am over this...."—as if everything about them is going to go back to the way they were before the trauma. Chances are good that they won't. Some things change us forever. The changes may be small and they may be positive, but the person who is waiting to get back to exactly who they were before could be waiting forever to move on. So, what is "healed" going to look like to you?

When you are in the depths of what feels like unending grief, there are steps you can take to make it manageable, to shrink it and carry it within you instead of letting it envelop you. Go back to gratitude. Focus on the time you had with the person you lost. Think about happier memories. Remember that they will always be with you in spirit and memory. The life you live can be a testament to that memory, a vessel to carry it forward.

See if you can identify what their life purpose and lesson may have been and how this loss fits in with that. *Death happened to them.* That was their journey. What you are dealing with are the emotions and loss created for you.

The idea that the life you live can be a testament to those memories ties in well with the concept of self-compassion. We spend a lot of time talking about self-esteem. We think about how we have to believe in ourselves and champion our own abilities. We talk about how to build self-esteem as a foundation for success in children. These things matter, but sometimes we spend more time talking about how to believe in ourselves than we talk about how to *care* for ourselves. Self-compassion is just as important as self-esteem, but it is not nearly so universally praised.

I ask my clients to watch Dr. Kristen Neff's TED Talk on the subject of self-compassion. She highlights the "importance of including ourselves in the circle of compassion" that we create in our lives. We need to treat ourselves with "the same kindness, care, and concern that we treat a good friend."

If you wouldn't say something mean to your best friend, why would you say it to yourself? If your best friend had a rough morning (let's say she spilled coffee on her shirt, which made her late to work, so her boss reprimanded her and told her she was on the verge of getting fired), would you spend the your time telling her she was irresponsible, undeserving, and doomed to failure? I hope not (or else you probably won't stay friends long).

Instead, you would take the time to point out her strengths, empathize with her frustrations, and lend an ear while she voiced her feelings. It's only after you give her that chance to decompress that she can step back and build a plan that addresses the underlying issues and create a better tomorrow. We have to start with compassion, and in our friendships we often know that instinctually.

The same rule applies to our conversations with ourselves. Dr. Neff explains that the problem with self-esteem is that it is "contingent on success." We have self-esteem only when we can find ourselves in a narrative of success, see ourselves as the champion of our stories. But there are times when we cannot find success. There are truly low periods in our lives when we can't read ourselves into that story, when things really are as bad as they seem. That's why self-compassion is such an important tool. You can be compassionate in the absence of success. In fact, compassion is often easiest for us to dole out to others when they are at their lowest points. If you can find that compassion to give to a friend in need, why can't you recognize when you *are* the friend in need?

Dr. Neff also points out that compassion is rooted in what connects us rather than what sets us apart. Self-esteem, on the other hand, is built out of differences. We have confidence in ourselves based on the ways we are different from others. We run faster, work harder, do better, and we find our worth in those ways we are set apart from the people around us. Self-esteem comes when we deserve the raise because we worked harder than our peers. We deserve the nice car because we earned more money. We deserve to win the race because we ran faster. To build self-esteem, we're constantly measuring ourselves against others and their accomplishments, and while that can sometimes lead us to seeing ourselves in a better light, it often leads to feelings of falling short. After all, we can't always be the fastest, the smartest, the strongest, the best.

Self-compassion, though, asks us to do the opposite. Instead of seeing ourselves in a competition with others, self-compassion asks us to see ourselves as connected to others in a universally shared humanity. Alexander Pope said, "To err is human, to forgive is divine." We often think about the need to forgive others their faults, but we need to remember to also forgive ourselves our own. Shame, blame, and fear are not strong long-term motivators. If we want sustainable changes, we need to start with compassion. Recognizing our own mistakes and the places we fall short puts us in with a pretty big crowd—we are right there with everyone else in the world.

Pay attention to how you talk to yourself. Words have power! Words have energy! If you're looking in the mirror and pinching your belly rolls while calling yourself a fat ass, ask if you'd say those words to your friend. If you miss a deadline at work and call yourself an idiot, imagine someone else saying that to your partner. You'd probably be quick to come to their defense. Be your own defense, even if the enemy is yourself.

I know a rabbi who said that instead of using negative self-talk, we need to use the language of our grandmothers. They never called us stupid. "Oh, sweetheart," my grandmother would say before telling me something that might have been hard to hear. "You're being silly." Never would she say, "You're being stupid." This rabbi suggested that when we make a wrong turn, we start with kind words, and then take a deep breath.

The only constant in this life is you. No matter where you go, you'll still be there, so building a positive relationship with yourself and cultivating a positive attitude about who you are and what your purpose is will go a long way toward making that journey more bearable. After all, sweetheart, you'll be in good company.

resilience road

beth koritz

Everyone is handed adversity in life. No one's journey is easy. It's how they handle it that makes people unique.

~ Kevin Conroy

Slow Movement Ahead

The lesson of cultivating a positive attitude and being mindful of the way I framed my own story grew out of years of following a path that wasn't entirely meant for me. It was a long, slow lesson that took decades to learn (and I continue to work on it every day). The next lesson, though incredibly difficult, was a focused one. I'd been broken by disease, and now I had to repair myself. It was time for recovery, and I would come out of it healed not just in my body, but also in my mind.

The first stop in my path to physical recovery was transitioning to a step-down unit. After that I would move on to rehab. The plan was for me to spend a few weeks in the transition unit, and as soon as I was settled in, my kids could finally come see me. They hadn't been allowed in the ICU, so it had been two long weeks since we'd laid eyes on one another. My daughters, their faces obscured behind paper masks, stared at me wide-eyed as I tried to explain. Their last image of me had been my body almost frozen in the hospital bed.

The first visit with them after I got out of ICU was an emotional one. I was still unable to move so I could not hug or hold them. When it was time for the babysitter to take them home, Dallas lunged forward and grabbed onto the bedrail with both hands, knuckles turning white from gripping so hard. "No! No!" she screamed. "I want my mom!"

Daniel picked her up and tried to gently tug her from the bed. It was no use. They had to individually pry each finger away, and she screamed the whole time. "I want my mom! I want my mom!"

I was trying so hard not to cry in front of her, and I couldn't even reach out to comfort her. As Daniel carried her down the hall, I could hear her screams fading as she got farther and farther away. It wasn't until they got into the elevator and the doors closed that I could no longer hear her calling for me. I burst into tears.

Just before their visit I had found out that the other mom from Dallas's class hadn't made it. I was thrust into an existential crisis. *Why her?* I remember asking myself. *Why not me? Why either of us?* I thought about her little boy, Dallas's classmate, waiting for his mom to come home. What would Dallas have felt like if I didn't make it back? How could a child handle something like that? It bolstered my resolve to get out of there as quickly as I could.

Up until that point I had been trying my best to take the diagnosis and treatment in stride, focusing on staying calm and stoic. But I was alone now, so I didn't have anyone left to be stoic for. I lost it. I was sobbing—for my kids, out of fear, out of frustration, out of grief for the other mother, all of it. I had yet to give myself the space to have a substantial emotional response, and everything had been piling up. It was a moment to process and release.

"It's going to be okay," a calm voice assured me.

What the fuck, I thought. *Where is that coming from?!*

"Who is that?" I asked the empty room.

The voice returned. "This is Penny at the nurse's station."

No one had bothered to tell me that I was being watched on a closed-circuit camera. I felt completely violated. My private moment of processing had become someone else's televised drama. I had needed that moment of cathartic hysteria, but instead I was jostled out of grief and plunged into anger at having been so violated and cheated out of a very private moment.

Recovery was a lesson in vulnerability. I was still paralyzed from the shoulders down, so I couldn't even lift my hands to hit the nurse call button. They put this round, rubber thing about the size of a silver dollar on the pillow next to my head. I was supposed to roll my head over and hit it with my cheek when I needed a nurse. Sometimes it would fall off the pillow, and then I was out of luck, completely unable to connect with anyone until someone happened to come by. I was already dreading spending the next few weeks lying there unable to have any control.

That's not what happened, though. About a day later, I was moved directly to the rehab unit. Apparently, someone had come in to evaluate me and had "seen something" in me even though I was barely able to move. I could twitch my right thumb at one joint. That's how they determined my fighting spirit was lying in wait. Here I was at my weakest, and without my realizing it, my determination was shining through. I was going to skip the step-down unit and go straight to the hard work of getting back control of my body.

The move to the rehab unit was really scary. The step-down unit was at one hospital, the same place I had been in the ICU. The rehab center, though, was at an adjoining hospital, so I had to be moved from one to the other on my bed. It felt like we had traveled across the entire medical complex to get from the tenth floor of the first hospital to the subterranean levels of the second. It took more than 20 minutes, and there was something very degrading to me about being whisked through the public hallways on a bed.

The first nurse who came to see me in the rehab unit was Sylvia. She was short and stocky, almost square. She had a tight Afro, dark with sprinklings of silver. She looked sweet, and she could be when she wanted to, but she took a tough love approach to seeing progress in her patients.

Only 4,000 cases of GBS occur each year in the United States. That means one out of 100,000 people contracts the disease. Someone put this into perspective for me by saying, "Imagine the baseball stadium being filled. Now imagine the football stadium being filled. Take all of those people combined and only one of them will get GBS." So it was not surprising that almost none of the people who worked with me in the hospital had ever worked with a GBS patient. I don't think Sylvia understood that there was no amount of willpower that was going to make my muscles move before the myelin sheath had regenerated. It just wasn't possible.

That didn't stop her from barking orders at me like a drill sergeant. "You're not on a regular floor now!" she snapped at me. "You're going to have to work hard here.

We don't put up with excuses!" It scared the shit out of me because I still couldn't move anything below my shoulders—unless you count that twitching thumb.

I was placed in a double room, but I was the only one in it. The floor was half underground with a tiny window at shoulder height. It was dingy and depressing. The thought of having to be in that room, peering out at the ground through the gloom as I tried to fight for my own body to move was too much. I felt depressed and scared. I found myself unable to find anything positive to focus on.

My mom went to bat for me. Another room on the floor was bigger and more private, with a kitchenette. This is where occupational therapists taught Activities of Daily Living (ADL) classes in the kitchen, helping people return to normal daily activities as part of their therapy. I'm not sure what strings my mom pulled to get me moved. All I know is that soon I was in this much bigger, brighter room. It had a table and chairs. The kids could come and do crafts and sit with me. A couch made it more comfortable, so visitors were much more likely to stay and mingle. I had a full-sized fridge that my mom kept stocked with her tapioca pudding and tuna fish that I'd eat on Wheat Thins (my greatest culinary pleasure while in the hospital). It was like going from a dingy room at the Bates motel to a mini-suite at a LaQuinta. My spirits lifted immediately. The change enabled me to start finding the positives and shifting my focus in that direction.

Every day after breakfast, I had one physical therapy session and one occupational therapy session. After lunch, the routine repeated.

Everyone had the same goal: to get me out of there. Everything was painful. My muscles were completely atrophied. When the physical therapist lifted my leg off the bed the first time, I screamed in pain.

"I've only lifted it two inches!" he protested.

I didn't care if he'd only lifted it a centimeter. It was excruciating!

Over time, though, I started to make friends with the staff. I joked that there must be some kind of rule that all physical therapists retire at 30 because I never saw one older than that. Kara was my primary PT and Kelly was my primary occupational therapist. We got friendly enough that we'd have lunch together. They'd wheel me in my wheelchair and sign me out to cross the Parkway to eat at Einstein's.

The work was hard. At one point my doctor came in and told me she was prescribing Prozac. I asked why, and she said that it was a prophylactic measure they gave to people dealing with chronic issues. I wasn't sure about the prescription at the time. I didn't feel depressed. But it was a good thing they gave it to me. Rehab was hard physically and sometimes excruciatingly painful, but the mental fight was the toughest.

They'd make me get dressed every morning and into a gown every night. The act of changing clothes was supposed to spark a sense of purpose and routine in what was otherwise an unbroken band of sameness. There was a nurse's aide who treated me like a side of beef. One morning before I had regained any movement, she was getting me dressed and flipped me over to get my pants on, jerking one leg up and then letting it drop back to the bed like she was tossing garbage into the back of a truck. She had no compassion for a living, breathing human being who could feel everything she did. Maybe my paralysis gave the false impression that I couldn't feel anything, but surely she knew I could hear her, and she didn't speak to me at all. It was so dehumanizing. I just shut down.

I couldn't find my voice. I was counting on these people for everything—everything. If I had to go to the bathroom, if I needed to take a shower, if I wanted to get dressed, if it was time to take my meds, if it was time to turn me to prevent bedsores—all of that was on them. These were the most rudimentary of daily activities, the things I'd always taken for granted as my own domain, elements of life I could control. Some of these were functions I'd had since infancy! I'd literally never been so helpless before or since. When you can't brush your teeth or even scratch your leg without assistance, you feel very small and vulnerable.

I had learned to be relatively good at standing up for myself, but I didn't have the strength to fight for better treatment. I felt like it would fall on deaf ears, and I had no power to follow through. What was I going to do if they didn't comply? And how might their annoyance with my complaints make my already dependent, fragile state even more vulnerable? I said nothing as this woman tossed me from side to side and turned around without ever having spoken to me. I just let it happen. As she marched out of the room to "help" another patient, tears silently streamed down my face.

I was so busy fighting the physical fight to bring my body back that I had no energy left to win the struggle to find my inner voice and use it to advocate for myself.

Eventually, I had to learn to ask for help. People see asking for help as a weakness but it's really a strength, a form of self-advocacy. I had to learn that I couldn't expect myself to be Superwoman. Nobody else expected that of me. Why was it okay for me to expect it of myself? *It is okay to be vulnerable.* Right after I was taken off life support and was still in the ICU, I had to poop so badly. (Yes, dear reader, I am so comfortable being vulnerable I am going to tell you about my poop.) My bowels hadn't moved in two weeks while my body was completely motionless. I couldn't even be propped up to use the toilet. "Just poop in your bed, and we'll come take care of it when you're done," the nurses told me. I was aghast at the thought.

The pain was so bad. Imagine being constipated as badly as you've ever been. When you're on the toilet, you can lean forward and backward. Gravity is your friend. You can rub your stomach, push your feet into the floor. I couldn't do any of that. I had been turned on to my side. I couldn't contract my muscles at all. The pain was so bad that I was screaming, groaning, and crying. My mom was standing there with me.

Here I was, 35 years old, and I had to have the comfort of my mother's hand so I could poop. So that I could poop in a bed and then lie there helplessly while other people cleaned it up. That was a *"What the fuck have I come to!?!"* moment if ever I've had one. There's nothing like that level of vulnerability to take you to an absolute baseline of defenselessness. It was almost like a reversion to innocence. It's like going back to being a baby, being stripped of all ego. But I was 35, and up until then I'd had a healthy ego!

For the next four weeks I was still shitting in the bed and calling a nurse to say, "Somebody needs to come clean me up." Every time I made that call, I knew that my words—my weaknesses—were being broadcast across the entire nurse's station. Then I had to lay there, completely aware but utterly frozen, as the nurses came to change the sheets and wipe my body clean. At some point it stops being embarrassing and becomes business as usual. It's very humbling. When we ask for help it often feels as if we are asking for the world and that the people we are asking are being put out or having their world rocked by our request. The fact is, when we reach out, not only is the helper's world not rocked, it is often just another normal part of their day. Better yet, they are often grateful for the opportunity.

I absolutely hated a couple of things about that hospital stay. The staff was very bad about turning me over to prevent bedsores. Multiple nights would go by when I wouldn't get turned at all. When my primary doctor found out, she was furious and demanded that the nurses pay more attention. I also had to wear the long compression socks that prevent blood clotting. The hose were so tight. One nurse would come in each night to strip them off, using a lotion that one of my visitors had brought to me from the Dead Sea. I loved the feel of having someone massage my weary legs and feet after they escaped those damned hose. No one else did that when that nurse had the day off. It was her small act of kindness, and it meant the world to me. Funny enough, even a whiff of that lotion now takes me right back into that bed, into feeling trapped and alone, but at the time it was a brief escape.

Another thing I hated was having to get Heparin shots in my belly twice a day to prevent blood clots. Adding it all up later, it amounted to 78 injections. My

95

belly took on the grotesque look of a swollen grape, black and blue and distended from all the abuse.

"What do I have to do to stop these?" I asked the doctor in desperation. It was time to stay focused on what I could control and the actions I needed to take.

She said I had to walk 100 yards twice in the same day. That was all I needed to hear. It was happening. I wasn't getting another one of those fucking shots.

An hour later Kara came to get me for PT, and I told her we were going to walk 100 yards, twice! I did it. That day (have I mentioned how determined I am?) I went four times around the PT room with a walker. I didn't care if I would be so exhausted afterwards that I'd have to lie in bed for days, but I wasn't getting another shot. Even though the walk was tough, I felt emotionally stronger right away.

"What do I have to do to get these compression hose off?" I asked, this time with more confidence. I had to walk even more, so I did that, too.

"What do I have to do to get out of here?" That was the big question, and it was a little more complicated.

One of my first big tests was Mother's Day. My mom had booked an ambulance taxi so I could go to my aunt's house for our annual Mother's Day celebration. They loaded up my wheelchair, strapped it to the floor of the van, and off we went. It was so awkward realizing that my wheelchair had been placed in the exact spot in my aunt's living room where we used to place my grandmother's wheelchair. It was disorienting and surreal. In those moments I did not feel like myself. Here I was, 35 years old, sitting where my grandmother sat, in a wheelchair just like her. It briefly took me back to feeling out of control and that my life wasn't my own. It was nice to get out, but it was emotional being driven back to the hospital. For a moment I had caught a glimpse of what I was missing outside of my bubble of therapy, pain, and boredom. The world was going on without me in it, and this day was a strong reminder of just how much I wasn't a part of it.

On the Fourth of July, there was no therapy. All of the therapists had the day off. It pissed me off to think that I was losing an entire day of progress. "If I'm going to be stuck here in this hospital, I'm going to be doing something to get me out of here!" I made enough of a fuss about it that Kara agreed to come in and give me one session of PT. That night my family went to the club as we did most years to watch fireworks and eat dinner. My mother picked me up and drove me to the club, and then my brother brought me back to the hospital. Once more, my taste of the life I was missing was brief and disorienting. My world was small and painstakingly focused on a single task: permanent escape.

There was a recreational therapist whose job was to teach patients how to handle being out in public. She came to me when I was first moved to the rehab unit and talked about field trips, but I was adamant that I didn't need or want to go. The wheelchair was temporary, I insisted, and learning how to use it in the outside world suggested I needed to get used to it, but I didn't want to get used to it. I was working too hard on getting myself out of it to think about needing it after my release.

Eventually, I realized that was a silly attitude to take. The wheelchair was temporary, but I also wasn't going to get stronger unless I challenged myself. I eventually agreed to a field trip to the art museum. My mom came along to wheel me around. There were about eight of us, and each patient had to have a designated person to assist them.

My mom accompanied me on another field trip, this one to the outdoor opera theater. There's nothing like being in a black wheelchair in a 95-degree St. Louis summer. I was stuck to my seat and dripping sweat. My clothes and hair were drenched. We were sitting way up in the wheelchair section. This trip had no redeeming moments.

The third trip was to Union Station. We had to use the MetroLink public transit system, which was so difficult.

Those field trips gave me an abundance of respect for those who cope with physical challenges on a daily basis. This world is not built for wheelchairs or walkers.

I was going to be released soon, so my sister came and took me to the mall to get some clothes to wear during recovery. I ran across a few acquaintances there who had no idea I had been sick. I remember seeing their faces when they saw my sister pushing me through the mall: it was horror. They saw me and immediately felt fear, dread, and pity. If it could happen to me, it could happen to anyone. I really didn't need to see those faces, to be reminded of how the world saw me in that moment.

A few days before I was to be released, my physical therapist, occupational therapist, and my mother took me to my house to assess what kind of adaptive equipment I would need and if there was anything else they needed to teach me for me to live in my own space in my current state. At that point I was using a walker for small efforts and a wheelchair for bigger ones. We had ordered a custom-built electric wheelchair since we could not be sure how much longer my recovery would take. My muscles would be very weak for a long time, so operating the wheelchair on my own wasn't realistic. Opening a jar of jelly wasn't even realistic.

When I got into the house and I sat on the couch in the same room that the kids had been in when I had been taken out two months prior, I lost my shit (figuratively). I started sobbing uncontrollably. It came out of nowhere with no warning whatsoever. I think that my mother and my two therapists were as surprised by the outburst as I was. Everything I had been through in the last two months just came crashing down on me as reality. How much of my life and my children's lives I'd missed. The horror of it all! I'd done such a good job of staying positive throughout the emotional and physical pain of the whole experience, but at that moment something in me just broke and the dam opened up.

My mom was sitting on the couch with me and the therapists were standing in the room looking around. In their eyes, being home was good news! This was what we had been working toward! It took me a little while to get it together enough to move back to the practical discussion of how I would live in this space.

The wheelchair we'd ordered would take a few weeks, so I was using one I'd borrowed from our nanny. I needed a nanny at this point considering that my kids were 4 and 7—and on summer vacation to boot! Luckily I had a first-floor bedroom, but they were on the second floor and stairs were going to be out of the question for a while.

I ended up recovering fast enough that we cancelled the special-order wheelchair. I was determined to be walking soon enough.

Little by little I regained my mobility. I pieced together my freedom from the restrictions I'd been living with for so long. Once I was close to being back on my feet, the world looked a lot different. I could broaden my focus from my immediate recovery needs to what I wanted my future to look like. I didn't have any more time to waste living a life I didn't love. I had said things needed to change, and the change would start now.

resilience road

beth koritz

Run with a heart of gratitude and you'll travel further than you ever thought you could.

~Anonymous

Bridge May Become Icy

I had been out of the hospital for a little under a year, and I was still returning for outpatient OT and PT services three times a week. You may not think your body can do much, but you don't really appreciate how much it is capable of until you're fighting to get every bit of capability back.

Despite still being in recovery, I was ready to get the ball rolling on the life I'd envisioned while trapped in that bed. I had recognized I was walking on a path that wasn't meant for me, and it was time to make a change and get on the right one, even if that meant clearing a path that wasn't there yet.

Right away, I knew we had to get away from the deli. It had become a constant source of tension in our marriage, a drain on our energy, and a physical reminder of how far off track my plan had gotten. We arranged to sell our share of the restaurant to our business partners, and I could feel a weight lifting off my shoulders with each step.

At the same time we planned a trip to New York to take the kids to visit Daniel's family. In my mind, it was a marker of our return to normalcy, a marker of my new start. If I could handle the travel, the kids, the busyness of it all, I knew it would increase my feelings of being in control of my life again.

The day before we were going to leave, we spent the morning signing the closing paperwork for the sale of the deli. That afternoon, I had a physical therapy appointment. It looked like everything was on track for a smooth start to our new lives. It was like I had glimpsed a sliver of my true path across the tangles of forest and underbrush from the wrong one I had been walking, and now I was finally about to cross out of the wilderness in between and get where I belonged.

I was ready.

My PT took me outside so I could practice walking on uneven ground. I wanted to say that I'd been on uneven ground for a while now, but the PT meant the literal kind, so I headed for the grass. I had grown much more confident in my abilities, and though my steps were slow, they were steady.

Until they weren't... I turned an ankle. I was lying on the ground looking at the sun above me, and I screamed the only words I could get out: "FUCK!" I must have screamed it to the heavens 50 times. "FUCKFUCKFUCKFUCKFUCK! FUCK!"

I had sprained my ankle so badly that my entire leg, ankle to thigh, turned black and blue. I wasn't just shouting out the pain of that moment; I was mourning the new start I'd been telling myself I would have. Once I saw what must happen, the changes my life needed, I wanted to put my determination to work and barrel through until I got there, but there would be no barreling through today. This was going to be a slower process than I wanted it to be, no matter how much I willed it to be otherwise. There were no shortcuts regardless of how hard I worked. This was a stark reminder to me that patience is an important part of the process of self-growth.

I wasn't strong enough and still didn't have enough motor skills to use crutches, so it was back into that damn wheelchair. My New York trip, my chance to demonstrate my recovery, turned into a wheelchair-bound flight, an inescapable reminder that though things may finally have been changing, they were doing so *slowly*.

We stayed with Daniel's parents in New York. They were fine and generous hosts, but tension always hung in the air when he was around them. I don't think he ever fully lived up to what they'd hoped he'd become. Being in their presence always made him shrink a bit.

The first night there he had what I called his "nervous breakdown." It was a full-blown panic attack, the first I had ever seen. Since I had known him, he had always been mentally stable and physically healthy, so it was shocking to see him collapse into such despair so quickly. The whole week we were in New York, he was an anxious mess. He had become someone I didn't recognize. Someone had flipped a switch and my husband had become a completely different human being.

I thought he'd return to himself when we got back home. Surely the travel, my condition, helping me to navigate the wheelchair and the girls while his parents' disappointments floated silently around the room had all taken a toll on him. We'd get back, my ankle would heal, the recovery would progress, and he'd go back to his old self, refreshed with the release of the duty of running the deli and ready to work with me to build the life we both said we wanted.

That didn't happen.

When we got home, his anxiety escalated. He became depressed to the point that it was debilitating. Looking back, our new business plan—which we had worked out together—must not have been enough. He must have felt like an unmoored ship, floating out amongst the unknown. He couldn't handle it. What if my new path wasn't his new path? What then?

Not working added to his downward spiral over the next few weeks. I would leave the house at 7:15 each morning—still struggling to regain my full physical abilities—and take the girls to school. I'd keep myself busy and out of the house all day long until it was time to pick them up because it was so hard to be around him. His negativity was toxic, especially when I was working hard to stay focused on positive thoughts about my own future.

I helped him get into counseling. He had a counselor of his own, and we were also seeing someone together. I was desperate to get the man I married back. I wanted him to walk my new path with me. I wanted this to be a journey we took together.

At one point he suggested that he might hurt himself. I called my father and asked him to take Daniel to the hospital. One of the girls had a birthday party to attend, and I didn't want them to know what was going on. I thought it was better that I get them out of the house and let my dad handle the work of getting him to agree to the hospital. Daniel agreed to check in, and he stayed for about a week.

We kept working on our marriage, but it was increasingly difficult. We decided to take the girls to Sanibel Island for winter break. We loaded up our Jolly Green Giant—a big green conversion van—and headed south. The drive was long, so we split it into two days. We arrived at a nice beachside place. I thought that this could be a healing trip. I was hopeful that this time together would provide some fun and relief.

There were some nice moments. The vastness of the ocean has a way of making problems seem smaller. Standing on the beach as a family, watching Dallas go into hysterics when a seagull stole her Rice Krispie treat right out of her hand, things seemed like they were okay— normal. Anyone looking at us certainly would have thought that we were a young family who had all of life spread out before us.

On day three of our seven-day beach stay, my parents called. One of Daniel's best friends had died quite unexpectedly. He had gotten an infection in his heart and was dead three days later. This was someone Daniel had gone to school with, who had been a groomsman in our wedding. We had spent a lot of time with him and his wife. He was a phenomenal human being. I knew that I would have to deliver the news gently because Daniel was, to put it mildly, still in a delicate state.

Anyone would have been overcome with grief to find out that one of his best friends had died suddenly. Being hundreds of miles away and knowing he had missed any chance to say goodbye just made it harder. He was adamant that he would attend the funeral. There was no way we would make it in time if we all tried to drive the

Jolly Green Giant to New York, so I started calling airlines.

The soonest he could leave was the next morning, but it would require a layover with a plane change. I wasn't at all convinced that he was in a mental state to handle the maneuvering on his own. I arranged for someone from the airline to escort him from gate to gate.

I was secretly hoping that sending him to New York alone would allow his family to see what was happening to him. I felt trapped with him in a giant bubble of anxiety and panic that no one else seemed to see. *Maybe,* I reasoned, *if I'm not there as a buffer, they'll see and help him get the help he needs.*

He stayed in New York about a week, and the girls and I finished our vacation in Florida. As horrible as it felt to admit, it was a lot more enjoyable without the ticking bomb of his anxiety and unease next to us.

We had a 24-hour drive facing us, and now I had to do it alone with the girls. I planned a stop in Chattanooga, Tennessee. We spent two nights in a hotel where you get to sleep in train cars, and we went to a truly amazing aquarium. These were some of the best moments of the trip, enjoying the company of my girls. Their energy and laughter were just what I needed.

Before getting sick, I had become a vegetarian, but I was still eating fish. In the aquarium I was surrounded by seven stories of glass aquarium walls. I watched those unbelievably gorgeous creatures swim by, and I thought, *How am I still eating you?*

I gave up fish and seafood at that moment. It's funny the things you remember, the way life hands you experiences when you're not expecting them.

Soon after, another excursion in the Jolly Green Giant offered the clarity I'd been trying to avoid. The four of us were driving to Vail, Colorado, for our semi-annual vacation there. We were in Kansas at night during a blizzard.

If the hugeness of the ocean had given us a moment where our problems were minimized, the stillness of the snow around us magnified them in the enclosed cabin of that van. As the world turned invisible around us, all I could see was what little was left of my marriage, magnified by the smallness of the space around us, and it simply was not enough.

We stopped to get something to eat, and while we were in the restaurant, we found out that the highway was closed to the west of us, with no hotels between us and Colorado. I decided to just power through. If we were stuck in the van all night anyway, I might as well get some miles out of the way.

It was blindingly white in the glare of my headlights, and no other cars to follow, no tracks to show us the way. They had put the arms down on the exit ramps, so we had nowhere to go but stay on the highway.

The girls were asleep in the back, and there was no safe place to pull over, so I was white-knuckling it at a torturous 10 miles an hour, slowly crunching the tires over the quickly-piling snow. I was envisioning how badly it could end. If we went off the highway, how long would it be before anyone could get us out of a ditch? A day? Two?

I was so stressed about staying on the highway, staying on the path that I wanted to be on, but I couldn't see the path. I couldn't see where the edges were. I couldn't see the median. I was driving blind.

It was the perfect metaphor for what was going on in my life. I finally knew where I wanted to be, but I had to travel on an untrodden path in order to get there, and the journey was scary. Fear wasn't enough to keep me from getting to the life I knew I was supposed to be living, though. Fear would not stop me from moving forward. Besides, I didn't really have a choice. Once I set my mind on the destination, there was no way to go but forward.

Next to me, in the passenger seat, my husband was not doing well. His anxiety had escalated, and he was adding to my stress exponentially. I remember thinking that I might as well be alone with the girls. *If something goes wrong,* I thought, *I won't be able to handle both his anxiety and my young girls.*

It dawned on me in that moment that this wasn't the partnership I wanted, the partnership I *needed.* It wasn't the deli. It wasn't my recovery. It wasn't his anxiety. It was us. I had been trying to blaze a trail to this new path with him by my side, compromising to make sure the new path would work for both of us, but *we* weren't working. I needed a partner I could depend on, a partner who was at least as strong as I am. I needed a partner that I knew had my back the way I had his.

As we were moving slowly down the highway with my nails digging into my palms, clutching the steering wheel, I muttered somewhat under my breath, "This is it. We're getting divorced." If Daniel heard me, he didn't acknowledge it.

It was my breaking point. I had just come out of this death-defying event. My only goal in life was to make memories for my family, for my kids, and I had tried everything I could to help him be a part of that. We had been to therapy together. He'd been to therapy alone. I'd been hospitalized for my recovery. He'd been hospitalized for his. Nothing was working, and it was only getting worse.

I wasn't quite ready to act on it yet, but I knew it was over. As I continued my drive through the night, the snow let up and I could begin to see the edges of the path I was traveling.

After returning home, we kept going through the motions of normalcy, but things were getting worse in the most insidious ways. We went on another few months this way, and one day Dylan looked at me while I was tucking her into bed and said, "I just want Dad to go away on vacation and come back and be better."

I had stayed in the marriage because I thought it was better for the girls, but her comment made me realize they were scared. His anxiety and behavior had infected the whole house. I told him he needed to move out and get better.

I packed his things, and drove him to a nearby hotel. After a few days it was clear that he wouldn't be coming back home anytime soon. I found him a nice three-bedroom apartment because I wanted him in a place where the kids could stay with him.

At this point he was continuing to deteriorate. I moved him in, went shopping, and bought everything he would need. There I was, standing in the aisle looking over plates and pots and pans—shopping for a home I wasn't going to live in, shopping for a home that represented the crumbling of my own. I focused on getting nice things for the girls' bedroom. I wanted them to feel comfortable at his place.

Technically, we were separated. He was taking the girls one night a week and every other weekend, but other than that, nothing was different. Eventually he became so passive that I felt the act of caring for them was more than he could handle, and I worried for their safety. I hated doing it, but I told him that if things didn't change, the girls wouldn't be able to stay with him anymore. He could see them whenever he wanted, but they couldn't stay at his place. I thought it would be enough to push him to change.

It wasn't.

Time passed. I asked him to meet me at the county library. We got two chairs in a corner by the window. It was private. There were stacks of books all around us, and no people in sight.

"This has been going on too long," I said. It had been nine months since that fated drive through the blizzard. More than a year had passed since my release from the hospital and my vow to make every day count. "I don't see you trying to improve."

I had gone straight from recovering from GBS to coaching him through this anxiety and depression. To some extent, I resented that he had watched how hard I had worked at my own recovery. Every step of the way, I had asked, "What do I need to do?" and then I did it. I didn't matter how hard it was, how much it hurt, or how frustrated I became. I didn't see him making that same effort.

I wanted to meet in the public library because I wasn't sure how he would react and I didn't want there to be a scene. "I want a divorce."

He didn't react much in that moment. We parted ways, and I called a lawyer.

He ended up seeking treatment and we put the divorce on hold so he could focus on his recovery. Even though the marriage was over, our love for each other was not. His recovery was as important to me as moving my and the girls' lives forward. After treatment I saw a big difference; he was pretty much a worn version of his old, better self. But I could not go backwards. Shortly after he came back, I called my lawyer. "Let's finish this." Back then we both had to go to the courthouse for our court date. The attorneys went in to the courtroom while we sat in the hallway to be available in case we were needed. We were sitting close to one another on a hard bench, chatting like old friends. It was Halloween, so every once in a while someone would walk by in a costume. One woman was a dead bride—complete with a wedding dress, zombie face with blood dripping from her mouth, and silver wig. I watched her walk past us, down the shiny hallway and looked at Daniel as she vanished from sight.

"You've got to be fucking kidding me," I said. "I feel like we're on an episode of *The Twilight Zone!*" We laughed together. It was like a dream. Surreal. Hazy.

The divorce was complete. He went to his apartment. I went home.

A few hours later, we both went to our friends' house where we'd taken the kids every Halloween. I stayed to hand out candy, and he took the kids to trick or treat. It was like any other Halloween, like we hadn't just gotten divorced five hours earlier.

beth koritz

There's no map for you to follow and take your journey.
You are Lewis and Clark. You are the mapmaker.

~Phillipa Soo

Road Trip

There I was. Therapy: complete. Divorce: final. Me: free.

I could do whatever I wanted without having to answer to doctors who scheduled my days, a husband who wasn't on my path, or a body that wouldn't hold up when I needed it to. Now was the time to finally push through and make sure I was on the authentic path I'd glanced from that hospital bed and so desperately wanted to be walking. Now was the time to start making those memories I had promised the girls—that I had promised myself.

Perhaps it is fitting that I wanted to feel confident in my figurative path by ambitiously tackling a literal one. I planned a 17-day road trip: St. Louis, Memphis, Nashville, Gatlinburg, Asheville, and Charlotte, where one of the girls' former babysitters was getting married. We'd stay two to four nights in each place then we'd drive back, stopping in Louisville.

I wanted to make memories, and that's what we did.

In Memphis we stayed at the Peabody Hotel and watched the ducks walk to the fountain. We swam in its spectacular indoor underground pool and ate at B.B. King's. I'd been a vegetarian for years, but Dylan ordered a cheeseburger and teased me with it, waving it in my face. "Mom! You know you want it! You know you want a bite!"

I was on this trip because my philosophy had changed. Life's too short to deny yourself experiences. I grabbed the burger out of her hand and ate half of it. It was the best thing I'd ever tasted.

The next night we went to a steak place and I ordered the biggest filet they had on the menu. I savored every juicy bite of it. Smiling, Dylan announced to the waiter that I had been a vegetarian the day before, knowing she was responsible for broadening my culinary horizon.

In Nashville we visited the Country Music Hall of Fame. At the Wildhorse Saloon we danced to the house band, and I taught the girls to two-step. I can think back on it and still imagine their smiles and giggles as we danced.

Every city had its own highlight. Each stop held something new. We were traveling the country, connecting the dots like a puzzle, growing closer to each other as we made our way toward the coast.

We were staying at the Opryland Hotel, and I wanted to let go and enjoy the moment, but the reality of our lives back home had followed us. I was selling the house that Daniel and I had built, that "sandcastle" that was unrecognizable as the home we'd planned together. I was running back and forth from the hotel business center, juggling the signing of contracts and letting my real estate agent know when we'd be in each city. This was before smartphones and emails. It was paper faxing and long-distance codes; it was a pain in the ass.

In Gatlinburg we stayed in a lodge with signs posted warning us not to go out at night. There could be bears!

Sure enough, we were driving down the little road to get to town, and a bear cub walked right in front of our car. We stopped when it was just a few feet away and watched it amble on—not an experience you'd get in St. Louis! In Asheville we went to the Vanderbilt Mansion, something I had done as a child with my own parents. It was marvelous to remember how I felt seeing this as a child while I was watching my own children experience it.

When we made it to Charlotte, all the other guests were beside themselves that we had driven all that way for a wedding. The bride loved showing off the girls, her little girls she had cared for. On the way back, we had dinner in Louisville with a friend I hadn't seen in 20 years.

By the time we got home I was exhausted. I don't know what I was thinking, taking two little girls on such a massive excursion. We were changing hotels every few days. Packing the bags, lugging them around, driving, lifting, lugging—and I was only just out of therapy for GBS.

Looking back, it was crazy of me to take on such a physically demanding and exhausting trip so soon after recovery. It was an insane thing to do.

And I'd do it again in a heartbeat. I wouldn't trade the stories and memories I made on that trip for the world. To this day, my girls—grown women now—will reminisce with me about that trip. The songs we sang along with on the radio, the hamburger, the dancing.

This, I thought, this is the way life is supposed to be.

This is what it is all about!

beth koritz

Happiness cannot be traveled to, owned, earned, worn or consumed. Happiness is the spiritual experience of living with love, grace, and gratitude.

~Denis Waitley

No Idling Allowed

Of course, life can't just be road trips and dancing, so I had to figure out how to start fresh when we got home and school started again. Being divorced was emotionally hard, especially since there weren't many models of it in my community. In Dallas's class of 24 kids, I was the only single parent. There were 23 traditionally married couples, and then there was me. At the time, fitting in was still incredibly important to me, and it was something I had struggled to feel successful at accomplishing even before the divorce. I had come a long way in this journey of self-growth, but I still had a long way to go.

My kids went to a private school, and its identity was clear. It was conservative, wealthy, and serious (everything I wasn't). I was surrounded by cookie-cutter moms wearing Lily Pulitzer and "doing lunch." I remember wearing a plaid Ralph Lauren tweed blazer that wasn't my style at all, but I'd often wear it when I had to go to school. I was trying to look the part, but I always felt a little off, stiff and uncomfortable playing that role. I should have known that just feeling that level of discomfort is a big red sign that I wasn't being authentic. I had grown up with some financial comfort, and even after the divorce I was still situated well. These people were not *way* out of my league, but they were playing a different game. I didn't want my kids' social lives to suffer, though, so I'd show up and act the part, trying to look like I belonged.

Now, post-divorce, I stuck out even more. I had to put on a front of having it all together, but the truth was that things weren't going so smoothly. I had a lot of financial and legal stuff to deal with, and I had to go through it all alone. I didn't have people to bounce the problems around with or blow off some steam. Most of my friends were Daniel's friends, too, and I didn't want to share what I was going through with them. I had my family, and they were amazing, but I felt lonely and alone.

The house was sold. I bought a comfortable home for myself and the girls. I was starting to get into my new rhythm as a single woman.

A few years after the divorce, I was at one of my brother's concerts. His band would play in St. Louis about once a year. During the show, I met a man named Kirk. He and I hit it off, and after the show we went to the adjoining bar to have a few drinks and get to know each other. We agreed to meet again the next day.

That was it. The pace was set, and we had a fast and furious relationship. He seemed like the antithesis to my ex. Daniel had always been a smooth talker and had the ability to blend into any social situation. Kirk was rougher around the edges. Looking back, I can see now that Kirk was my rebellion, my way to signal to the world that I could conquer it all, that my setbacks wouldn't actually set me back. That I was done trying to meet society's or anyone else's expectations for my life. *I'm going to show them all*, I'd think to myself.

Who were "they?" Well, everyone! Every school mom who (I thought) looked at me like I didn't fit in the room. Every person who was shocked that my "perfect marriage" hadn't actually been so perfect. Every acquaintance who wouldn't meet my eye when I was wheelchair-bound. All of them! But really—it was me who needed proof that my story had many more chapters, that I hadn't crashed and burned at the midpoint, that starting over didn't mean giving up on having the life I wanted. I needed a statement that solidified my "new" life, but in some ways the ghost of that old checklist was still hanging on.

People wondered what I was doing with Kirk. They'd tell me that he wasn't right for me, that I could find someone who fit me better. That just made me all the more determined to make it work. I was forging a new path and I was determined that it was different than the path I had just been on. Early on, we had a ton of fun together, and it was exactly what I needed. After years of struggling to recover the strength of my own body and then struggling to keep our lives together as Daniel fell apart, I wanted to have fun.

Kirk was great for fun. He paid a lot of attention to me, which was a real stroke to my ego. I also kept telling myself that he was the opposite of Daniel, and that was exactly what I thought I needed. We'd run off for weekends to a cabin, go to concerts, and have other adventures. After feeling like my life had been in a holding pattern, Kirk felt like the partner who would be by my side through life's adventures. I was enthralled with the idea of being with someone I saw as so completely different.

He had a temper, though. Even though he was tough on the exterior, he was also sensitive. His feelings would get hurt easily, and that would lead to defensiveness, which in turn led to anger. He was always somewhere in the cycle, and it would start to feel like holding a ticking time bomb. I was never really sure when it would go off.

I also knew that I didn't really want to get married again. I didn't need it. Being independent had many advantages. He would bring up marriage intermittently, and I would always brush it off. We were having fun. Why ruin it? He started bringing the girls into it. They're young, he'd say. It'll be better for them if we're married, if things are stable.

I gave in. I didn't give in because I thought he was right. I gave in because I was tired of being the strong one, the one who makes all the decisions. I had spent the last few years building a home and raising my children virtually by myself, going through the trauma of my illness with Daniel's illness quickly following. I had gotten divorced and had to rebuild my life on my own. It had been exhausting. I wanted to just let things happen, to go with the flow and see where the path would take me. I didn't want to work so hard to create the right life all the time.

Getting engaged was very anticlimactic. We had bought rings that were sitting in a drawer. I woke up one day and said, "What are we waiting for?" Then I put on the ring myself. That was the engagement story. There was no special moment to it, no memories to cherish. So different from the first time.

I still believe that going with the flow and allowing life to happen can be good, but we can't abdicate our responsibilities and give up all control over our paths. That's what I was doing. I wanted to be weightless, free of the burden of being responsible for my own life. That's what Kirk represented. But I wasn't paying attention to that big red sign. Just a few days before the wedding, while driving down the highway I said aloud to myself in the car, *I shouldn't do this. I wish one person would tell me that I don't have to go through with this.* But no one did, and I was in an unfortunate time-out from taking personal responsibility.

My children weren't crazy about the idea of Kirk as a stepfather, but they were young enough (7 and 10) that they accepted it without too much protest. I had friends traveling into town for the wedding, which was only a few days away. I didn't want to go through with it, but I thought of how embarrassing it would be to cancel so close to the big day. I was back in that trap of being worried about what people would think, and I didn't want to prove all of those early naysayers right. I was not honoring my inner voice. I ignored what I knew was the right decision.

At the same time, I woke up with a big black spot on the middle of my nose. I went to my dermatologist, who said she would need to do a biopsy. I wouldn't let her because I was getting married in a few days and didn't want my nose to have stitches. My friend who did my makeup for the wedding spackled layers of concealer over the black spot. At the party afterwards, one of my cousins kept trying to wipe the "dirt" off my nose. I never did find out what it was, but it went away on the honeymoon.

I now think that it was a sign, a physical manifestation of what I knew to be a mistake. My body always has a way of letting me know when I'm on the wrong path.

The marriage lasted for four years, but it broke down pretty quickly. We had one decent year, one mediocre year, one bad year, and one horrible year. The last year of our marriage we barely spoke.

The actual defining moment of our separation is so petty as to be almost cliché. Have you heard the saying that marriages fall apart over arguments about how to load a dishwasher? Yep, that's what actually happened. He was loading the dishwasher, and I walked behind him and said, "You could fit more dishes if you put the pan this way." Suddenly we were standing on separate sides of the kitchen counter and he was talking to me through clenched teeth. I could see his jaw pulsating with rage. It seemed as if he couldn't unclench it. That was the first time I found myself thinking, *He might hit me.* He never raised a hand, but I had never been afraid of him like that before.

"I'm going for a walk," I said suddenly. I grabbed my jacket and stormed out the door. At one point, I thought, *Oh no! The kids are in that house with him!* But it was a fleeting thought. I knew he wouldn't hurt them. I walked for about an hour, and I ran through everything in my head. I made the decision on that walk that it was really, truly over.

He was calm by the time I walked back in the door. "We need to talk," I told him. "I'm done." We sat down and pounded out our separation agreement right then and there at the kitchen table.

Watch for Falling Rocks

The marriage hadn't worked out, but during that time I had the opportunity to change careers. I had found something engaging and interesting. When Kirk and I married, I was working as the director of a day camp. I worked with Sara, whose husband built houses. I had grown up working at my dad's home improvement store, so I knew much more than your typical suburban Jewish girl about building supplies. My parents even gave me a workshop in my basement for my 30th birthday, and I'm talking about power tools, not glue guns.

I had been heavily involved with the building of the house that Daniel and I lived in, and I had built a large addition onto the house that Kirk and I lived in. I'd also consulted on additions and remodels for other people. Building houses seemed like a great next step for me, and at the time it was a lucrative option.

I introduced myself to Sara's husband, Frank, and asked him if he needed any help. He had just started a new project, so he couldn't take anyone on at the

beth koritz

moment, but I asked him to keep me in mind the next time he had something new.

About two weeks later, the financing fell through on the project he was working on, so he called me. We made an agreement. We'd split the profit fifty-fifty. Frank would be the general contractor, and I would be in charge of securing the loan, the general design work, and the business end of the deal.

It seemed like a perfect fit. Kirk was a master carpenter, so he could make custom cabinets and doors and make the place stand out. We were creating high-quality, unique homes that were gorgeous. Frank got a business partner, I got to do something rewarding and creative, and Kirk got work to support his struggling business. Win-win-win. Our first house sold well. Shortly after that, Kirk and I got divorced.

I realized that I didn't need Kirk to continue the work. It was refreshing to have something that carried me through the transition. Unlike when I divorced Daniel, this time I still had my life intact. I wasn't starting over because I had continuity in what I was doing professionally and had strong friendships outside my marriage. Kirk was no longer walking the path with me, but I was still on the same path. The right path. My path.

Frank and I built and sold another house on our own. There is something so rewarding about watching an idea in your head go from a project in progress to a finished product to money in the bank. It was like selling dreams.

As we were working on our third house, the economy started to look a little iffy. This was the middle of 2006. Still, we knew that this kind of work comes with some risks. Things were looking up overall. Then the housing bubble burst.

We were about 90 percent finished with the third house and had put it on the market. But, St. Louis isn't a place where people often buy before a house is completely finished. It takes a lot of vision to see what a home under construction will look like when it's done. We were putting the finishing touches on the house while hoping it would sell before completion. The clock was running out as we saw the news reports about the housing market falling apart. Then the proverbial roof caved in. The bank called in the construction loan before it was due. I had no way to pay it without the house selling. I had guaranteed the loan with stocks in my portfolio, and they called it all in. They froze my assets and took over the property. They took everything.

Well, everything except the tax burden from the bank selling off my stocks. Between the state and the IRS, I had a $40,000 tax bill and no way to pay for it. They had cleaned me out. I had been depending on my profit from the house sale, and it wasn't going to happen. There was no easy way to put it: I was flat broke and in big debt.

How would I raise my kids? Where would the money come from? In addition to the tax burden, I had tons of credit card debt from vendors and suppliers we had used to build the houses. They wanted their money. One day a friend of mine—a man I had one date with as a teen and who now lived nearby with his wife—gave me a courtesy call. He was a processor, and he'd noticed my name in his pile of subpoenas to serve.

"I didn't want to just show up at your house and surprise you with it," he said sheepishly. "When would be a good time to come by?"

There I was, standing in the doorway of my nice home, opening it for a man I knew, who was handing me a paper we both knew said I was a failure. I was humiliated.

I felt angry at everyone. I was angry at myself for chasing the dream of this career. I was angry at the banks for betraying me. The entire time I was trying to work with the bankers, they would lie to my face. They'd say they'd have to take the negotiations "back to the office" when we both knew there was no further conversation happening at the office. They were just trying to pass the insult and injury on to some non-existent entity so that they could keep smiling to my face.

It was hard to be a woman in that business. Even though I was the one doing the financial backing, the bankers would often speak only to Frank despite the fact that I was sitting right there. It was unethical and infuriating. I found out that not long after the bank seized my assets and the property that it went belly up. Its desperate act had destroyed my life but hadn't saved the bank.

I was still financially entangled with Frank and his wife, Sara, my former co-worker. She was a 50-50 partner on his part of the business, and we were still partners on the last house as it went through foreclosure. Just the year before we had been together when the second house had sold and gone out to celebrate. There was no celebrating now, but we were still wrapped up in each other's lives.

I didn't tell anyone what was going on other than my parents, my brother, and my sister. Definitely not the kids. I didn't want them worrying about how our bills would be paid. Dallas was 14 and Dylan was 17—old enough to understand what was going on. I didn't want that burden or stress on them. Still, I was a mess. I was crying all the time, terrified, panicked about finding income. I had gone from feeling I had control over my life to feeling no control and living in fear. This had been my full-time job. I didn't have any other income, and even though I had worked in some amazing positions, I didn't exactly have a stable résumé that pointed me toward a specific career path. I'd always taken opportunities as they came, but to an outsider my work looked like it was all over the map.

I talked to Daniel about what was going on with my finances, and he also felt that we shouldn't tell the girls. He said he would help me until I was back on my feet. It was above and beyond what an ex-husband needed to do. He did it because he's a great father and wanted to protect his girls.

Things weren't going well, but I was holding it together. Then one day, Daniel called me. "Beth, I want you to hear it from me before you hear it from anyone else." I didn't have time to figure out if I should feel afraid or curious. "Sara and I went out on a date last night. We had a lot of fun. I think I'm going to ask her out again. I just wanted you to know."

I couldn't even wrap my head around what he was telling me. All I could choke out was, "It's too close." But he wasn't listening. What I was thinking was, *Are you fucking kidding me? You're dating her? My friend? My business partner's wife? Right now?*

It hadn't occurred to me at the time that she was the one who orchestrated it all. She had asked him out. I called Frank and found out that they'd been separated for a few months. I was still actively talking to Frank several times a day to deal with the foreclosure and still getting financial support from Daniel. It was just too much entanglement to handle.

My girls were pissed and hurt when they found out that Daniel was dating Sara. Then it got really bad. Suddenly things that I had told Frank in confidence as a friend many years earlier were coming up in arguments he had with Sara. Daniel would get angry that I had been talking to Frank about our past, even though it was years ago when I had no idea Daniel and Frank would ever know one another. Still, he was mad about it. I was terrified he would cut us off financially. If he did, I'd be on the streets.

The drama of it all started making me physically ill. I was having off-the-charts migraines, and I was crying all the time, completely unable to control the tears once they started. I was driving home one day when a thought bounced through my head as if someone else had tossed a ball. *Wouldn't it be nice if I just wasn't here to deal with this?*

I didn't want to die. I didn't want to hurt myself. But in that moment, I understood people who said they'd thought these dark thoughts before. I was just so overwhelmed by my reality that not existing had appeal. It was a shocking thought to find in my mind. This was not me. *Things would be much easier if I just weren't here anymore.*

It scared me. I had never thought anything like that before. I called my doctor right away. "You need to give me something. I can't stop crying." We made a short-term plan, and I started to feel a little better, a little more in control. I had taken action.

I decided the only way out of this mess—and I mean *all* of that mess, the money and the interpersonal drama—was to file for bankruptcy. I started interviewing attorneys. I interviewed three, and each one was either condescending to me, told me something I couldn't bear, or wasn't compassionate in any way. I was coming to them at one of the lowest points in my life, and I wanted to be treated like something more than a paycheck and a series of numbers walking through the door. Thinking about hiring one of these people made me sick to my stomach.

This was not something I was going to settle on. I met with a fourth attorney. I felt like I had found someone who could really help me and understand what I was going through. Once I hired her, the ball got rolling. She helped me save my house. Through it all, I had never missed a payment. There wasn't enough equity in the house for it to be worth anything to the bank anyway. I got to keep my car because I owed as much as it was worth. My credit cards were gone. Overnight I went from having no financial worries to worrying about paying for groceries. I was limited to the cash I had on hand. It wasn't much.

This is when the girls figured out something was up. Their lives had been changing as rapidly as mine during this period. I had to take their cell phones out of my name and put them in Daniel's. They started to piece this change together with my crying jags. They had thought I was just upset about Sara and Daniel, but now they realized it was bigger than that. I told them I was having some financial trouble. I didn't tell them it was bankruptcy until many years later.

I didn't tell anyone about it. In many ways this was every bit as traumatic as the GBS had been. I felt just as vulnerable and in need of support, but I was also ashamed. I was never ashamed of being sick—who can control what their body does?—but this felt shameful. How had I let this happen?

Looking at it now, I know that every builder in the city—hell, across the whole country—was going through the same thing. Bigger, smarter people than me went down harder than I did. Experienced people who knew the risks and the industry much better than I did made the same choices. I couldn't have done anything to stop it even if I had seen it coming. I had the house. I had the car. Everything else was beyond my control. Now all I could do was wait for the dust to settle.

It had been *years* since I woke up in that bed and decided that my life was going to change. Life had changed all right, and I had grabbed some memories and experiences worth hanging onto. I had learned many lessons and things about myself. I had worked on honoring my authenticity. But this was another setback on the path to living the life I wanted to live. It was time to start over... again.

Tools for the Road Construction Ahead

As you can see from my story, there was a point in time I tried to place blame on the world around me, on the things happening to me. I now understand that never works. I believe we are all 100 percent responsible for everything we do: thoughts, emotions, and actions.

It can be hard to get to a place of understanding our own responsibility, though. The natural tendency is to look outward instead of inward, to find something else to carry the burden of our disappointments and pain. This is especially true during our darkest moments, when the deck seems stacked against us.

We often start with making excuses when we take actions we are ashamed of taking or that otherwise don't match our goals and values.

"I ate that giant piece of chocolate cake because my boss was so mean to me today and made me sad."

"I didn't call my friend when I said I would because the last time I saw her, she was rude to me and hurt my feelings."

"I didn't submit that job application today because my partner made me so angry this afternoon." And if we take that idea of personal responsibility one step further, we have to realize that the next guy is also 100 percent responsible. If we agree that we all have 100 percent responsibility for ourselves, then how can you feel guilty for how someone else feels? What percentage does he have open for you to be responsible for him? There is no room for you to be responsible for another person's thoughts, feelings, or actions.

While we are not responsible for how someone else feels over something we have done, we do need to take responsibility for our original action. Will you look back and think that you regret your actions? I tell my clients that their goal should be to look in the mirror at the end of each day and be able to say "Today I was the best version of myself." Perhaps one day you will look in that mirror and say, "I regret the way I spoke to my friend. I need to apologize and work on that." That's you taking responsibility for your actions without taking responsibility for the feelings that she chose to have.

Forks in The Road: Blame or Responsibility

In these cases, we are trying to excuse our actions, but in order to do that, we start placing blame on others for our own emotional processes. We're acting as if these feelings are something happening *to* us. As if we were just walking along, going about our day, and fell into some anger like we were falling into quicksand. We give our emotions too much power when we don't recognize that we can control them.

Control begins with understanding and validation. If we stop and think about our emotions, really examine them like artifacts on display in a museum, we'll see that they are tied to some thought. And thoughts don't come into the world on their own. They come from within us.

If they come from within us, then we have the power to change or stop them. Harnessing control over what we do with our thoughts—including changing them completely when we need to—is the first line in taking responsibility for our entire lives.

We try to change the actions we don't like, and when we can't, we blame the emotions that we're feeling. But we rarely strip the process all the way back to its origins: the thoughts we think.

This isn't entirely our fault. The world isn't set up in a way that makes us stop and listen. Our culture isn't designed for contemplative observation of our own thoughts. We're designed to be busy, to stay busy, to throw ourselves into the hustle and bustle to demonstrate our worth, our value.

It has gotten to the point that people wear busyness like a badge of honor. We brag about how few hours of sleep we need to function. We joke about our caffeine runs in the morning to keep us wired. We bring home stacks of work from the office. We send emails on vacation.

We're also bombarded with images, sounds, and sensations that take us outside of ourselves and remind us of our supposed obligation to society as a whole.

As we make our morning commutes, we're smacked with billboards reminding us to buy our groceries, whiten our teeth, flatten our bellies, invest in our portfolios, and buy some sparkly new jewelry because our busy selves deserve it. The radio fills our world with jingles so we always remember which brand of laundry detergent to buy and what fast-food drive-through to frequent since we obviously don't have time to cook.

We come home to relax by turning on a television that flickers from ad to ad while we scroll on our phones and compare ourselves to our friends' carefully curated timelines. There are perfectly manicured lawns to create, cupcakes to decorate, children's pictures to take in just the right pose. We scrutinize how many "likes" we get on a photo while wondering what it means if that person we just met doesn't accept our friend request within the hour.

From the time we wake up until the time we fall exhausted into bed, we have very little space for reflection and quiet contemplation. If we want that space, we have to make it, carve it out like a secret cave on a cold, treacherous mountain climb. The world we live in will not offer us a reprieve on its own. If we want the space to think, it is our responsibility to create it.

Even once we've done all of that, though, the work isn't over. We can start with recognizing the undesired action, work our way back through the emotion to the thought that started it all, and still not know what to do to change it.

I had a client who recognized that her thoughts were sabotaging her goals, but she still didn't know what to do with the thoughts. "How can I stop thinking about how much I hate my body?" she asked.

To some extent, you can't expect to totally eliminate thoughts. They're going to pop up like mushrooms from the ground after a rainstorm. We're awash in messages from the outside world, and we can't entirely stop them from implanting remnants of themselves in our minds. Thoughts we do not want to have can continue to appear. Expecting ourselves not to reflexively have a thought that has been ingrained in us, a thought that may have been comfortably making a home in our mind for decades, is setting ourselves up for failure.

What we *can* do, however, is catch that thought when it appears. We can recognize it, acknowledge where it comes from, and then correct it.

We do that by taking responsibility for what we do with the thought once we notice it. We have to recognize the thought for what it is: a product of our own mind. It's not some sacred truth placed before us like a hurdle that cannot be cleared. It's not some prophesy that dictates how we must live out the rest of our days. It's just a thought. It is a thought that our own minds created, which means it is a thought that our own minds can change.

We have the responsibility to shut those thoughts down, to bend them and twist them and shape them into what we want them to be.

The Clearer Path

The more we take responsibility for the thoughts in our own minds, the less they appear unbidden into our consciousness. On the flip side, the more we ignore them and refuse to examine where our actions and emotions originate, the more the unwanted and unhelpful thoughts replicate, spreading out like dandelions overtaking a field.

It's almost like protecting your water source from poison. You wouldn't dump poison into your drinking water, so why would you allow these thoughts to cloud your brain with toxicity?

Every time we find ourselves blaming someone else, we need to recognize it. We need to take a step back and see the bigger picture. We need to remind ourselves that no one else can make us feel or think or do anything.

If you find yourself saying that it's someone else's fault that you're angry, step back. If you say, "You make me so mad," step back. If you say, "You make me so sad," step back.

We are human. If someone insults you (intentionally or not), your gut reaction may be to be hurt, angry, or sad. But it's up to you and the actions you take if you are going to stay that way.

If the barista at Starbucks screws up your order and you don't notice until you're already on your way to the office, do you let that ruin your day? If someone cuts you off in traffic, do you carry that frustration with you all day? If your partner says something hurtful, do you hold onto that grudge like ammunition for the next argument?

There are lots of ways to stop this pattern. One of them is to find humor in the dark moments. Look for ways to laugh at the situation, the absurdity, the frustration. It's a lot harder to hold a grudge if you can find a way to laugh.

Another way is to look for the lessons. Everything happens for a reason, but that doesn't excuse us not being active in finding the right path. Did the Starbucks mess-up teach you patience? Is this an opportunity to turn to compassion? It can be as simple as this: *I've been finding ways to not let the little things get to me, and that barista just gave me an opportunity to practice.*

Some of my signs for recognizing a thought I need to change are:

- Do I feel out of control?
- Do I feel like my emotions are driving me rather than the other way around?
- Am I blaming somebody else for my problems?

The blame isn't always placed on another person. I have had religious clients who carry around grudges against God. Some people see the Universe itself as out to get them. Blame is a tricky sword to wield. Sometimes it hones in on a single target with precision and drives too deep. Other times it bounces around from target to target trying to find a surface to pierce. In both cases, we're using it to ward off our own responsibility. *The scariest idea of all: what if we are in charge of how we are feeling?*

I start by looking at my life. Are there patterns to the moments I feel the lowest? Are there triggers that plunge me into anger, guilt, self-pity, or blame? Are there certain people who always seem to push my buttons?

Once I recognize the power I've been giving a situation or a person, I ask myself, *Why am I letting them have this much control over my life?* After all, they're not the ones living in my shoes. I'm the one on this journey day in and day out. Letting someone with only a small role drive the day-to-day story of my life is a recipe for unhappiness.

Changing requires us to go right back to the same theme of responsibility. Once we recognize where we are currently channeling the power in our lives, we can work on getting it back, putting it back into the hands of the only people who can really change it. Ourselves.

For every situation that leaves you feeling drained, frustrated, and used up, ask yourself, "What piece of this do I own?" Sometimes, in a particularly long-standing power struggle, you may find that you own very little.

Maybe you have, over time, given up most of your power, but you are still in charge of how you react to the interaction. Nothing and no one can ever take that power away from you. If you can't find any other place to start, start there. "How will I react in this moment and how do I choose to handle that reaction?"

Once you begin and truly examine the patterns that make you feel out of control, you may soon recognize places of toxicity in your life. Maybe it is in your relationships or your work environment. Maybe you have to take hard, long-term steps to get yourself out of some of these situations. Perhaps you have to let go of a toxic "friend" who always brings you down, or maybe you need to quit that job and start a new career.

These are scary revelations. These are the things we've been hiding from. These are the reasons that we wielded our sword of blame to begin with. It's a lot easier to lash out at the world around us with "their faults" than it is to take stock of what we really want out of our lives and take the steps to get it; but it's only once we set aside that sword of blame and take responsibility for ourselves that we can start the work that must be done.

resilience road

beth koritz

In the long run, we shape our lives, and we shape our-selves. The process never ends until we die. And the choices we make are ultimately our own responsibility.

~Eleanor Roosevelt

Looking for the Right Turn

My heart was in the right place. I had followed someone else's script for my life and wound up on a path that wasn't meant for me, it was a path decades in the making. At this point in my journey I had forged some new paths with unintended results. We all believe that when we make choices they are the right ones. Why else would we make them? But just because a choice doesn't turn out to be the success we envisioned it being does not mean it was a mistake. The lessons learned along the way, what we learn about ourselves, and the elimination of possibilities are all integral pieces of the journey.

My path was about to take another turn. I was about to take another chance. I was looking through a local magazine called *The Healthy Planet*, and I saw a full-page ad about a seminar that was coming up. "Manifest your dreams," it said, and that sounded pretty good to me.

Of course, I had no business paying the $500 price tag when I wasn't sure what my financial future would look like. *You can't afford that*, I told myself. I turned the page, but then I turned back and looked at it again.

I took the magazine over to my computer and Googled the name of the person doing the seminar. *Look it up and prove to yourself that you don't need this*, the practical voice in my head was telling me. *Fine, but you still can't afford it.* It was true, but I had this buzzy feeling in the pit of my stomach. I was supposed to know about this. I tore the page out and slid it under the keyboard. *No harm keeping it around*, I shot back at that nagging voice.

I came back to that ad a few times over the next couple of weeks as I tried to figure out my next move, but then one day the nagging voice got the better of me. I kept wanting to call, but I didn't even have an idea yet. How can you ask someone to help make your dreams come true when you have no idea what your dreams are?

Shortly after, a business idea did come to me, though, and I was so excited about getting started that I didn't think I needed the ad anymore. *Dreams are for sleeping. It's time to take action!* I crumpled up the ad and threw it away. I was ready to get going!

I started an eco-consulting company called Green It! This was before the "green" movement really went mainstream, and I was one of the few individuals taking on the task in the St. Louis region.

A couple of months into what I thought was shaping up to be a pretty successful career, I was at my daughter's school to volunteer in the school bookstore. It was the beginning of the school year, so a new volunteer was partnering with me. We were chatting and getting to know one another, and it suddenly dawned on me that this was the woman from the ad. This was the woman I had Googled to find out more about how to manifest my dreams.

I'm sure she thought I was a little crazy, but I started freaking out. What are the chances of that happening? I started telling her the story about how I'd kept her ad under my computer until I'd thrown it away, but that I couldn't stop thinking about it.

"I'm doing another seminar this weekend in Kansas City," she said. "If you want to ride with me, you can go for free."

You'd think that would be the kismet ending of a cute story, but as luck would have it, I wasn't free that weekend. Perhaps it wasn't meant to be after all. Besides, I was on a new path to success. I didn't need help manifesting my dreams; they were already on their way to coming true.

After our shift at the bookstore ended, we went out to lunch. It was a nice day, and we were sitting outside. Planes kept flying overhead because we were near the regional airport.

"My husband's a pilot," she said. "He flies out of this airport."

"That's funny," I said. "My uncle flies out of here, too."

We got to talking about it and figured out that her husband and my uncle were actually flying partners. When I left the lunch, I called my uncle to tell him about this crazy coincidence with this woman who kept popping up in my life.

"Beth," my uncle said. "I'll do you one better. While you were sitting there having lunch with her, I was having lunch with her husband!"

Synchronicity is amazing and awesome to experience. There was a radio segment on *This American Life* about coincidences. The host said that some people ascribe too much meaning to what is really just a statistical anomaly. Guests on the show were talking about how weird it was to run into the same set of strangers multiple times in a day. A man giving a fake phone number to get away from a mall survey rattled off the surveyor's own number. A Thanksgiving dinner with extended family twisted through side topics until the guests realized that an inordinately large number of them all have 23 letters in their names.

Does it mean anything? Most people scoff and say it doesn't. "It's just a coincidence." It doesn't have to set the world into motion or make you change your life, but it can act as a kind of guardrail, and push you in the right direction just when you're looking for one.

After that interaction, I just knew there was a reason this woman was put into my life. A few weeks later, she called to say that she was giving another seminar. The cost of admission had given attendees the chance to bring a friend along for free. She had one person who didn't have a friend available to bring with her. Did I want to go?

I literally got tears in my eyes. At this point, the seminar had been on my mind for months. I felt like it just kept coming up over and over again. Now I was being offered the chance to go to a $1000 seminar for free through the kindness of a complete stranger. This was supposed to happen. Synchronicity.

The seminar itself was amazing. It introduced me to the idea that we can manifest our own lives, but the most important development was that my friend mentioned she was leading a year-long mastermind course. I signed up. She became my mentor, and that relationship offered paths forward when it looked like I was stuck. The mastermind group introduced me to women who are still very important to me today. It introduced me to the entire concept of energy, manifestation, and the law of attraction. Other than my graduate degree it is the most life-defining thing I have done in the past 10 years.

In many ways, that mentorship helped me grow Green It! with great success. I became the local CBS affiliate's go-to person and I was asked to speak on panels about environmentalism.

I would meet with businesses and individual homeowners to show them how to make their spaces more environmentally friendly and save money on their utilities. It was a lot of legwork. I was cold-calling businesses to set up lunch-and-learn workshops where I could educate employees. I inspected homes and taught owners how to conserve water and energy. I also started selling products to help meet those goals. I built relationships with vendors and built contacts in the local green community.

My visibility reached so far that someone in Atlanta reached out to see how she could get involved in my company. I ended up selling her a franchise. I co-wrote a book called *Eco Solutions 101*. It was a series of checklists people could use to bring eco-friendly principles into their lives and homes.

I was doing something meaningful that I enjoyed and I had respect among my like-minded peers. I was receiving attention from the community at large, and I was constantly busy moving between the different tasks of running a consulting company, which meant that I was never bored. There was just one little problem: I wasn't making money.

Utility bills in St. Louis are low enough that most people just don't give a damn about saving 10 percent on their heating and cooling. They'd bring me in, have me look over their homes, and maybe make a few minor alterations, but there wasn't a push for the kind of big changes that would make the company profitable. *It'll pick up*, I'd tell myself with every new consultation, every television appearance. *It has to!*

By this point I was nearing the end of the yearlong Mastermind program, which was focused on women in business. We met for three weekends that year, and had weekly conference calls as a group. I also had a one-on-one monthly session with my mentor.

The program met in St. Louis, so the commute was easy for me, but other people traveled from all over the country to make it to those meetings. The woman who ran the group had an energy that was clearly central to bringing us all together. Watching her have such a big impact on people wasn't just personally inspiring, it was also sparking something innovative in me. I found myself having lots of advice and guidance for the other women in the group. She suggested to me that this might be a natural talent of mine and that perhaps I could become a coach.

I could coach people! I took a hard look at my life, and I realized that the common thread between all of my job-hopping was my drive and individual vision. I left each thing I began because I got bored, and the work was no longer fulfilling, not because I couldn't do it or didn't do it well. If what I really wanted was the challenge of building something new, why not make a stable career out of a position that let me continuously build new things? If I were coaching other people through their own business decisions, I would get the energizing thrill of seeing something new appear and take flight, but I would also have the stability of a long-term career. I started looking into the credentialing process and the work it would take to get clients, and I was working on building it up slowly. I developed the "MAP Method:" Momentum + Accountability = Prosperity. I put it up on my website, and it's still there to this day. Although I have moved my primary focus from business coaching to counseling, this interest is still out there, and it's a skill I bring into my practice whenever it is helpful for my clients.

When I began, I had a few clients, and things were moving smoothly for them. I wasn't sure how to gain the momentum that would make this a full-fledged, profitable career, but I loved the work I was doing and found it fulfilling. At the same time I was concerned about not having a stable income and knowing exactly how much money I'd be bringing in from week to week. In the midst of this exploration and new moves, it was clear that Green It! wasn't going to be the answer to my financial problems. I started scheduling fewer and fewer consultations and phasing it out.

This search for my path was exhausting.

I began allowing fear over lack of money to creep in. I dipped back into some negative patterns, thinking that maybe what I really needed was to just find a job where I could clock in at the beginning of the day, clock out at the end, and leave it behind when I went home. Maybe I wanted the grind after all, and the ability to let the ins and outs of the job become someone else's problem for a change (had I learned nothing?).

I wasn't even asking myself what I wanted to do or what would make me happy anymore. It became a matter of practicality rather than goals. I'd see a job listed and think, *I'm qualified to do that.* At the time, all I wanted was to find something I could slog through for 20 years and retire. The nagging voice had grown quite loud: *Who cares if you like it! You need a paycheck! You need benefits! You have kids to take care of!* This place of fear was limiting my focus of possibilities.

For some of the jobs the competition was pretty fierce. I was applying to work in positions like director of a nonprofit teen program focused on cultural diversity, or directing the local office of a national health nonprofit. In two cases, the final interviews came down to me and one other person. They were both jobs I had rationalized were "good enough." I wasn't particularly excited about them, but I was like an animal in a trap. I was willing to gnaw my leg off if it meant I could get away from the constant fear and worry.

My fear of lack, of not being able to provide for myself or my children, was leading me off my authentic path and I knew it. But that same fear was keeping me from being able to self-correct. What would it take for me to conquer that fear and stay on my authentic path? As it turns out, the Universe was helping me with that.

I didn't get either job. At the time it felt like just one more defeat, but looking back, I thank God that I didn't. I know that, out of fear, I would have accepted a job and worked as hard as I could to be successful. I was never one to pass up an opportunity. But these opportunities would have only served to detour my path again. I could have easily been trapped doing a job I didn't like for decades, and jobs you start out not liking can turn into jobs you downright loathe.

Once again I could have made the mistake of walking the wrong path just because it was well-paved with other people's expectations and definitions of success. What felt like a setback at the time was really just the Universe's way of putting me where I needed to be once again.

I also knew that while I was searching for where I was supposed to be, I needed to make money to survive. I might have been picky about what I would be doing forever, but I wasn't picky about what I was doing right now. Through my green connections with the eco-consulting business, I found out that a friend needed help running the recycling for the Taste of St. Louis festival. By "running the recycling," what she really needed were people who would sift through the trash cans and sort out all the recyclable material that people had mistakenly or neglectfully thrown away. The pay was $10 an hour. In the heat, the stink, and the grime, I sifted through barrels of trash, amazed at all the expensive meals people had taken two bites of before tossing into a can to rot.

I've always had a survival-based work ethic. Even though I can get bored and move on, I always make sure I have something to move on to before I leave. I've always felt like there is *something* that can be done, even if it's digging through trash for $10 an hour. I tried hard to make sure my frustration over feeling stuck didn't translate into actual helplessness. Beneath every other message I've sent to myself, one has run quietly in the background: *You gotta do what you gotta do.* In other words, take action!

153

Throughout this seemingly endless saga of applying for jobs I didn't really want, forcing myself through the interviews, and ultimately getting rejected, I'd been toying with the idea of going back to school. Every time that voice in my head had plenty of reasons that this was a bad idea. *It's way too expensive! Even if you could afford it, you're too old to be sitting in classes with a bunch of twenty-year-olds. What would people think?*

Other than the deli, which we had owned for 10 years, I had never been in one place for more than four years. I had spent my life transitioning from job to job, from plan to plan. I didn't feel like a failure, but I assumed that others *saw me as* a failure. (Which of course, if I'm being totally honest, made me feel like a failure because I still cared about what other people thought of my life choices.) I could hear their hypothetical voices ringing in my head. *There she goes again. Why doesn't she stick to anything? Why can't she keep a job?* Even though I have never been fired and have always made the choice to move on voluntarily, I still felt the sting of these (assumed) judgments. If I was projecting to the world that I was flighty and couldn't commit to anything, maybe it was true, I reasoned.

I pushed the thought of school out of my mind by telling myself I was too old and it would just confirm these invisible critics' image of me.

I was so worn out and tired of putting all of myself into the start of something new only to have it not be the answer. If every effort had been a failure, I could have moved on quickly to the next thing and kept the momentum. If one of them had been a blinding success, I could have grabbed ahold of it and gone for the ride. Instead, they were all just okay. I was successful with a couple of direct sales products that I loved, but got tired of the grind of home parties. The repetitiveness of it bored me after the first year.

Every venture would start out as an exciting challenge, and I would pour myself into it, waiting to see if it picked up steam or died down. I was open to everything—anything!

I wasn't going to let anything pass me by, and I was sure that being open to anything the Universe presented would lead me to where I was supposed to be, a rewarding career that would last. Instead, it just kept along at the same lackluster pace and I would get bored when the challenge wore off. I was watching the years of my life melt away without finding the fulfillment I craved. I was so tired of doing all this fighting just to keep my head above water. I was approaching 50. Wasn't it time for me to find the rhythm of my path instead of all the starts and stops that had been happening for decades?

All the fighting in my head wasn't just taking a physical toll, it was also taking mental and emotional tolls as well. If we are not listening to our inner voices, if we are not paying attention to not just what is possible but also what is *right* for us, we can spin ourselves in circles until we are too worn out to recognize the right path when we do find ourselves on it. We have to push all the noise aside and just listen. Boy, had I been spinning! Now it was time to get quiet. Quiet enough to hear myself.

An acquaintance happened to make a Facebook post that she was going to a dream seminar. She wrote that the person leading it had been on Oprah. She got to bring a friend for free and was looking for someone to join her. I didn't even know what the event was about, but I messaged her without a moment's hesitation and told her

I was in. I wasn't sure if we were talking about the dreams you have when you're sleeping or life dreams, but I was open to everything. When I showed up that day, a couple hundred people were there, and I knew at least 10 of them. I had accidentally landed among my people, and I felt right at home.

Most of the seminar was one-on-one work in pairs. The facilitator would pose a question, and we'd pair up with a stranger to work through our responses. It was a brilliant move because I felt completely honest and willing to be vulnerable with a stranger. What did I care? I'd never see this person again if I didn't want to! For the next question, we'd switch partners.

At one point I was sitting across from a woman whose name I don't remember. I never saw her before or since, but she was there to witness one of the most important moments of my life. I had an epiphany, with tears streaming down my face. I finally was certain about what I really wanted to do with my life and, more importantly, what was holding me back. I wanted to work with people, and I would need more credibility to make coaching work long-term. I also didn't just want to help people start businesses and sell things; *I wanted to help people be the person they wanted to be. I wanted to take the lessons I'd been learning about living my own life and use them to help other people live theirs.*

The facilitator asked another question: "If you could do anything right now, what would it be?"

The answer flew into my mind. "Go back to school and not have to take a job based on how much it paid."

"What is keeping you from doing that?" the facilitator continued.

Suddenly I knew I was going back to school. That voice came back, and the same list of excuses started to fly. *I'm too old. I can't afford it. What if I try and it doesn't work? What if I don't like it? What if I'm not good at it? What will people think of me doing something completely new at this stage in my life?*

I had an answer for every question. *I'm only 48. I still have, hopefully, 30 good working years left in my life! I know I can qualify for student loans. I believe in my soul it will work, but if it doesn't I will take a life lesson away from it. If I don't like it, I will find something else. I know I'm a good coach, so I'm confident I'll be a good counselor. Most importantly, if this makes me happy, I'm not going to care what people think!*

With those answers, I was able to quiet that critical inner voice. This was the path. Everything had been pushing me toward it: the serendipitous meetings, the random acceptance of invitations to mysterious workshops, even the job rejections. I was being gently prodded to where I was supposed to be.

I was going to be a social worker. The next day, I was elbows-deep in applications. I had to apply for financial aid, fill out the forms, and write the admissions essay all in a matter of days. Classes were starting in two months!

It was amazing that my logical problem of needing to find a sustainable and rewarding career found its solution in such an alternative space. Most people have a clear dominant side between the left and right brains, but I don't have a dominant side. My right brain and my left brain often compete to see which side can be louder. This is both a blessing and a curse. The blessing is that I have interests that span the whole continuum. I'm very business-minded and goal driven, but I'm also very spontaneous, artsy, and free-spirited. I'm a true Aquarian.

Full of a renewed and much-needed sense of optimism and promise for the future, I quickly realized that I had missed the deadline to apply for the social work program... by one week. I began clicking furiously around the site. No way had I come this far, made this decision, and jumped through so many hoops to have to wait another year! This was meant to be! I was ready to start now!

As I explored the descriptions of the programs whose deadlines hadn't come, I found the counseling program. The more I read, the more I realized that I hadn't understood the differences between social work and counseling. The counseling program talked about learning to work one-on-one with people to help them cope with life's problems. It talked about counseling them through their lowest points and helping them to see better futures.

Well, shit, I said out loud to the computer screen. *This is what I wanted to do in the first place!* If I'd applied to the social work program, I would have been learning about something I didn't want. I could have *again* started off on the wrong path. Coincidence, or the Universe looking out for me again?

Even though I knew I was on my way back to school, I still needed a job. As luck would have it, another random Facebook post guided me. Someone on my feed had posted about a job opening for a part-time person to run a youth program. I was dialing the phone before I even finished reading it.

When the woman picked up, I launched into my pitch to try to land the job. "Hi, this is Beth Koritz, and I . . ."

She cut me off. "Of course! Beth! I know who you are."

That wasn't part of my script, so I was thrown off. How did this random woman on the other end of a phone at a place I'd never been know who I was?

The week before, horrible tornadoes had hit Joplin, Missouri. The destruction had been the topic of national news, and one of the local temples had asked for volunteers to come to the area and help out. I drove a U-Haul loaded with supplies to help those who had to relocate. The rabbi had included my name in a Facebook post thanking the volunteers, and I assumed that this woman had seen that post. She knew who I was even though I had no idea who she was. She set me up for an interview. (I found out later that she first learned about me when I had GBS. This was a reminder of how my illness, being so rare, became a story that spread like wildfire. Mine was the kind of story that people would hear and gasp, thinking how scary it was that it could have just as easily been them instead of me—a cautionary tale.)

Three weeks before, I had taken my daughter in to get her nose pierced. While she was getting it done, I thought, *That could be cute on me!* But then I said out loud, "Is there a point where you're too old to get your nose pierced?" The piercer said, "Absolutely not!"

I went home and thought about it, and I went back the next week. I was finally at the point in my life where

I was going to do what I wanted to do without worrying what people had to say about it. I don't know if I would have had the balls to do that a few years before. Now my resolve to do something and not worry about what other people thought was going to be put to the test. My brand-new nose piercing and I had an interview.

For a minute that nagging voice was back. *Just take it out! They won't see you as a professional interviewing for a job with a nose ring! You're a grown woman!*

Fuck it, I said to the empty room and to that voice in my head. *If this is the right job for me, they'll have to take me for who I am.* This was a huge thought for me. I couldn't have imagined not worrying about what other people thought of me and my choices a year before. Or at any other time in my life, for that matter.

The interview went well, but there was another finalist for the position. It would be perfect for me while I was in school because I would get to make my own hours and I didn't have to account for my time hourly. I imagined myself on the job, running the youth program part-time. I was sending out everything I could to the Universe to make this happen, something I hadn't done for other jobs I'd failed to land.

I was excited when I got the news that they'd selected me, but it didn't feel surprising. It felt right. It felt so right that I still do that job to this day. In fact, I just had my eight-year anniversary, making it the longest job I've ever had!

I'm very autonomous and work best on my own because I like to make a list of goals and get them done. In my downtime I can be pretty damned lazy, but not when it comes to work. It all balances out that way.

I'd dreamed, manifested, seminar-ed and action-ed my way out of the trap. Now I had a job and the promise of a new career on the horizon. I just had to suck it up and go back to school.

beth koritz

We all have our paths in life we are supposed to follow to find who we are supposed to be, but it's not always a straight path. There is something inside of us that guides us, and if you are quiet and listen to it, you'll be all right.

~Kyan Douglas

Making a U-Turn

I applied to University of Missouri-St. Louis (UMSL) and Webster University, but UMSL wasn't going to send out acceptance decisions until two weeks before classes started. That was cutting it too close for my comfort level, so when Webster sent me my acceptance letter, I registered without a second thought.

I did one semester at Webster. It was *horrible*. My very first class, Introduction to Counseling, was taught by an adjunct professor who, as it turns out, didn't like women, especially strong women. He was incredibly condescending to everyone in the class, spending most of the class time impressing upon us his own greatness. There wasn't a single class where he didn't take the opportunity to remind us of how great he was at what he did. It seemed to me that if he was so great at it, we'd be able to tell without him pointing it out.

Just as I started school I began having cluster migraines. I was put on a medication that can affect cognitive abilities. Here I was, one week into a graduate program, and I couldn't spell words that had more than four letters in them. I'd sit and stare at the computer screen after typing the first two letters and wouldn't know what to do. I would try Googling the first three letters to see which words came up, hoping for the one I wanted. Even the most basic of vocabulary words were beyond me. It was like my IQ had dropped by half overnight.

I was already self-conscious about being an older student on campus, and now I felt like I couldn't work to the best of my ability. I was taking three classes, a full load for a graduate student, and I was feeling completely overwhelmed because of the migraines and the meds.

The second or third week I was sitting in a class looking up at a PowerPoint presentation. I looked around and realized that everyone else was taking notes on printed copies of the presentation. I was frantically trying to write down every word on the board and every word the professor said, but I couldn't keep up. *Where did they all get the paper copies?* I went up and asked the professor afterward.

"They're on Blackboard," she said succinctly.

"What's a Blackboard?" I asked, confused. The last time I was in college, I had to type commands in code on my computer to make it operate. There was no Windows OS and there was certainly no Blackboard. I had taken the orientation for students, but at no point did the instructors explain how to access the technology. It was already 3 weeks into a 10-week semester, my brain felt like mashed potatoes, and I was beginning to wonder if I had bitten off more than I could chew.

A week after that, I'd adjusted to the medication, so the cognitive fog cleared and I was able to function like my old self. But the migraines were still there. My doctor increased the dose, so I had to start the whole process again. Just as I was able to think and spell again, I was right back to feeling like I was looking at the world through a sheet of gauze.

In the meantime, the condescending professor was getting worse and worse. Students would gather during the break in the middle of class to whisper about how unprofessional he was: "Holy shit! I can't believe he said that!"

Later that semester my cousin passed away from a sudden and surprising brain tumor. He was six years younger than me and had two little girls of his own in addition to being Dallas's godfather. It was devastating. I was sitting in class waiting for a phone call for an update on his status when I got a paper back. I was disappointed with the grade, so I went up to show the professor my outline for the next paper in the hopes of improving my scores.

I had put a lot of work into the outline. "This is all wrong," he said callously. This class went from 6-10 p.m. I'd been working all day, waiting for the phone call to tell me my cousin had passed, and was just completely spent. I started crying.

"Oh my God!" the professor gasped. "What is *wrong* with you?"

I pulled myself together and told him about my cousin and the migraines. "What are you even doing here?" he asked me without a hint of concern. "You should really rethink even being in this class."

I left the room determined to prove him wrong. I went elsewhere for help on the paper. His words had lit a fire under me. *Fuck you!* I thought. *This is what I'm meant to do, and I'll be damned if you're slowing me down!* Discouraged with how Webster chose to handle this problem professor, I transferred to UMSL. I had already been accepted, so all I had to do was enroll in classes. I started there two weeks later, never missing a beat.

The switch to UMSL turned out to be the best thing I've ever done. The program was amazing, and I immediately clicked with the professors and the students. I went full time three semesters a year for two years. There I was, finishing my master's degree. I was nationally accredited and licensed to practice. It was a real accomplishment that was a ton of work, a ton of time, and a lot of juggling. This was one of the proudest moments of my whole life.

resilience road

We get to grow and change over time for a reason. It's rare to just wake up one day and move to where we want to be. It takes time. It takes risk. It takes missteps. It takes mistakes.

~beth koritz

Be Prepared to Stop

It felt like fate had put me on the fast track. I'd spent so long after the divorce and the housing market crash feeling like I couldn't get started again, feeling stuck in a life I didn't recognize as my own. Once I found this new path, things started clicking so fast, it felt like confirmation from the Universe that I was going in the right direction.

As soon as I graduated from UMSL, I was offered another program to coordinate at work. I also knew that I wanted to go straight into my own private counseling practice. I was too old to spend years working for someone else first. *I'm 50. If not now, when?* I decided to go for it. The new program at the agency allowed me the financial stability to take the risk to do both.

I was off and running, renting space by the hour to see clients and working two part-time jobs. Things were picking up on all sides. I was busy but happy.

Just a few months later I went to a conference in New York for one of the programs I coordinated. I was there with the people who ran Camp Sabra. As I mentioned, I'd been there for 14 years growing up; my family and I were still very active in their alumni group. The director of the camp also happened to be one of my closest friends. We decided to travel together to the conference along with two of her assistant directors.

While waiting at the gate for our flight home, she got an email informing her that the person she had hired to supervise the area directors was breaking their contract. She had a position to fill immediately because camp started in just eight weeks. She promptly asked me if I would be interested in the position.

We weren't seated together on the flight, but she and her colleagues passed me notes trying to convince me to accept the job.

I told them there was just no way I could fit something else on my plate right now. They kept slipping me notes begging me to take the job. They had the flight attendants and the other passengers in on it with them. I was literally getting messages from all sides urging me to make this move.

I felt apprehensive about it, and I could think of a million reasons not to take the job, so I started listing what perfect conditions would have to occur for me to say yes. I assumed as soon as they heard the list, they'd back off and realize I wasn't the right person.

I told them that I couldn't do it unless I could come home two days a week to see clients. My counseling practice was still brand new and I couldn't risk losing momentum. Building my business was my priority. The director said it was no problem. Check.

"I have a music festival I've been planning to attend for months. I can't miss it. I'd miss the beginning of staff training completely," I countered. No problem. Check.

Everything I wanted, every other excuse I threw at her, she batted down. Check. Check. Check.

It was a good chunk of money for 10 weeks of work. I could drive back to St. Louis for two days out of the week to see my clients so my business wouldn't get left behind. I wouldn't get a day off for 10 weeks, but so what? It's 10 weeks. I could do it.

Memorial Day weekend I went to the music festival and got to camp four days late. Four days later, it was the last night of senior staff training. To celebrate, all of the staff were going out for dinner by boat. It was a calm Sunday night on the lake without another boat in sight. We hit a little wave at just the wrong angle, and the boat vaulted upward. I bounced up, crashed back down on my seat, bounced up again, and crashed down hard.

I heard a loud pop as I landed with my left knee on the floor of the boat and my right leg sprawled across the seat. I knew right away something was seriously wrong. The pain was instant and spread like fire across my back. Everyone else around me was laughing because they thought the bouncing boat had been so fun, but then someone realized I wasn't getting up.

"Are you hurt?"

I couldn't even answer; I was in so much pain. It hurt so much I couldn't breathe.

The other passengers quickly realized it was serious. We returned to the dock so I could be taken to the infirmary. With some help, I struggled my way off the boat, but I was having trouble breathing through the pain. I looked up the hill I'd have to climb to make it to the infirmary. There was no way.

The property manager was a first responder, and he was on his way. He asked if I wanted an ambulance, but I was nervous about scaring the staff. After all, at this point I was still planning to be their supervisor the next day (yes, this is another time I didn't use an ambulance for the wrong reason).

"It's just a muscle spasm," I remember saying to the property manager. "Just take me to the infirmary and get me some ice and a muscle relaxer." He maneuvered me into his car and drove me up the hill. He gave me an ice pack and some topical numbing spray. Then he said he had to leave to pick up his kids. I nodded and assumed I was being left with some camp medical staff. I didn't realize they weren't there at the time.

I lay in the bed by myself for over an hour. The pain wasn't letting up, and I realized it wasn't just a muscle spasm. Something was really wrong. I also realized no one was coming back to the infirmary that night.

Two staff members who had just arrived at camp were hanging out in the room next to me. My loud moans and cries scared them out of the building. Now I was truly on my own. I texted the assistant director, who was at dinner, asking what I should do if I needed to go to the hospital. He told me he would send a car if I decided I wanted to leave. Half an hour later, I texted him again. I couldn't handle the pain anymore. I needed to go to the hospital.

He messaged back saying a senior staff member was on her way and would drive me. I'd never met her, but at this point I wasn't going to be picky. "Great," I responded.

A few minutes later, he messaged again saying she was off-site eating dinner. She'd be there afterwards.

I don't know why I didn't just tell him I needed an ambulance. Wait, yes I do. Again, I did not want to draw attention to myself or admit how bad this could be. It was a replay of an old pattern. I didn't want to make a big deal out of me.

I'd been writhing in pain by myself for more than an hour when suddenly everyone appeared at once. Here was the doctor, who had apparently been on-site the whole time but hadn't been notified about my injury, the new senior staffer who was there to drive me, and another staffer who showed up to check on me. What did I want to do?

The answer was clear: "Go to the hospital!"

Somehow they got me into a wheelchair and then into a car. The ride to the hospital in Jefferson City was absolutely excruciating. Every turn or bump sent waves of daggers up my spine. I was praying out loud to just pass out.

I didn't make the connection at the time, but looking back on it now, I see the terrible symmetry of this painful bumpy ride out of camp and the one I had made as a spider-bitten child. Once again, I was leaving immobilized and scared, unsure of what would happen next. Whether in your teens or in your fifties, feeling out of control of your own body and what will happen to you is terrifying.

We got to the ER, but five people were ahead of me. I had to wait. I was crying, moaning, and groaning in the wheelchair, arching my arms under me and pressing down on the arms of the chair to try to take the weight off my back.

Finally checked in and after five doses of morphine, my pain was still at a level five out of five. I was taken to X-ray, where the tech asked me to move to a gurney. I couldn't do it. He took matters into his own hands. "In my experience," he said, "this is best done quickly." Then he jerked the sheet like a magician doing a trick, and I fell abruptly from the hard metal of the gurney to the X-ray table. I have never felt such pain before or since.

Back in the ER the doctor read the x-ray and returned to my room with the results. "You have a burst fracture to your L1."

I asked, "Will I be able to be back at camp by session break?"

He lightly chuckled. "You won't be doing anything for a very long time."

That was the moment I knew that this was another catastrophic setback. This wasn't just a bump in my road. This was a serious road block.

I hadn't gotten to the hospital until 11:30 at night, so after my diagnosis I didn't call my family. What was the point of waking them in the middle of the night when there was nothing they could do?

I was transferred to a regular hospital room where I lay alone and awake all night thinking about having to deliver this news to my parents and children. At 6 a.m., I thought if I called my mother and let her know, my head might clear enough for me to get a little sleep.

The situation seemed ominously fitting for what was becoming my personal Memorial Day theme: misery and immobility. Once again, incidents in my life seemed to be mirroring one another. Here was a second summer that I would spend flat on my back, largely immobile. Here was another moment of my adulthood where I would be thrust back into child-like dependence. Once more my path toward success was waylaid.

For years after my GBS experience, the approach of the holiday weekend had made me uneasy. I was in my doctor's office every May with an ache or a pain that had me concerned.

Finally, the doctor pointed out the pattern to me, and I realized that the reaction I was having wasn't to anything current. It was a reaction to past trauma. I would be flooded with the memories of every time I felt most vulnerable and fragile.

Once I was able to recognize the connection I was able to identify the source of the anxiety and allow my rational self to recognize that these were really just little aches and pains that I probably felt all year round. It was just the fear imprinted on me from the past that made them seem so serious. I had to learn to take responsibility for those thoughts, not only for my own sanity but to avoid creating a self-fulfilling prophecy. But here I was again. Clearly I had more lessons to learn and changes to make.

The next thing I knew, I opened my eyes and my sister was standing over me as I squirmed in pain.

I wasn't sure how my sister had gotten there. I hadn't even told her about my broken back yet! But my mom had called her, and she was immediately out the door and on her way to Jefferson City. I was so happy to see her.

A doctor came in. "Why'd you break your back?"

I must have looked perplexed. *What kind of fucking question is that?!*

"I mean, do you have soft bones or something?" he went on.

"No. My bones are fine!" (I had actually had a bone density test three months before, so I knew this to be true.)

"Well, this is bad. I mean, this is really, really bad. The kind of bad that's going to affect you for the rest of your life bad." His delivery was unbelievable. "I haven't looked at or worked on a spine in 30 years, but the spine guy is on vacation. I'm in orthopedics and I'm pretty sure we can get you fixed up by injecting cement to the injury site."

My sister and I both shouted "No!" at the same time. "We're going to St. Louis." An orthopedic surgeon friend gave me a referral. That doctor wanted me transferred from Jefferson City to St. Louis by ambulance. But you guessed it, no ambulance for me. I told him my sister would be driving me and I'd be in his office the next morning.

The Jefferson City hospital staff made a back brace for the ride home, but it turns out that it was the completely wrong kind of brace for my injury. It probably made things worse.

When the doctor came into the exam room to see me the next morning, I had tears running down my cheeks from the excruciating pain. I could actually hear the tears plopping onto the paper on the exam table.

"I bet you wished you'd used that ambulance, huh?" he asked.

I just nodded.

"Let's get you to the hospital."

I nodded some more.

The next day I was fitted with a proper brace. The (somewhat humiliating) fitting process meant covering my naked torso in wet, cold papier-mâché. Then I had to lie still and wait for it to dry. I was once again immobile and vulnerable in a hospital bed with my mother by my side.

After three more days in the hospital I was sent home with instructions for a long recovery.

I had been at camp for four days. What was supposed to be the beginning of 10 weeks of crazy, frantic busyness became an involuntary hard pause. I lived in my parents' house for 14 weeks. It was October before I got the back brace off. I had taken on way too much, let the siren song of other people's plans for me call me until I was in way over my head, and the Universe had taken care of it all for me. I had known that taking on the camp job was too much, but I chose to do it anyway. This was a clear message: *Slow the fuck down.*

My family lived too far away to help me on a daily basis. So, my big transition back into having control over my life came to an abrupt end when I was 50 and living with my parents. When I finally made it back to my own house, I still had months of physical therapy ahead to get back on my feet.

Okay, Universe. I thought. You win. I'm slowing down now. I'm taking time to pause and find peace in my life instead of being on a mission to always propel myself forward.

Apparently, the Universe needed to make sure I was *really* listening.

In October, while I was still in physical therapy for my back, I went in for my annual mammogram. "You need to schedule a biopsy," the technician said. "There's something on the scan."

The techs say it so casually, which I guess makes sense for people who do cancer screenings all day long. Maybe they forget that what's routine for them is life or death for you. I went in for a biopsy the next week, and a woman called me back with the results the same day.

That can't be good, I thought. No one calls you that fast to tell you they found nothing.

"You have cancer."

The dagger of ice to my heart was still running its way through my veins as the woman on the other end of the line ran through the next steps with all the efficiency of a well-written grocery list. "We'll need to see you in the morning for an MRI with contrast. Your appointment is at 7:30. We've scheduled you to see an oncologist on Friday." Beneath the nonchalant tone of her voice was the steady clip of a gallop. *Hurry, hurry, hurry. There's no time to waste.*

My sister had been my rock when my back was broken. She had gone to every doctor's appointment with me, and now four months later it was happening again.

We'd been in and out of doctor's offices, hospital waiting rooms, the rush, rush, rush of needing treatment punctuated by the pause, pause, pause of waiting. Always waiting. Waiting for results. Waiting to be seen. Waiting for the next plan with her always by my side.

I was weighing my options, and I was leaning toward a bilateral mastectomy. I'd get a reconstruction from my stomach. It was a 10-hour procedure and a grueling recovery period, but I didn't have a lot of options.

My primary doctor felt strongly that I shouldn't have radiation treatment. The spot was too close to my lungs where I'd had the sarcoidosis. She didn't want to risk agitating an area that had been problematic in the past. Getting a breast removed seemed like the nuclear option, but maybe nuclear is the right path when it suddenly feels like you're wearing a part of your body like a ticking bomb. You want the threat as far away from you as you can get it, even when the threat is part of you.

The decision was heavy, but I didn't agonize over making it. I was worried about the recovery—both the physical and the mental adjustments to my new body—but I was more concerned with making sure I stayed healthy. I made my decision.

Before surgery, the hospital runs the laboratory tests again when the original tests were performed by an external lab. I was sitting in my oncologist's office to tell her my decision about the mastectomy, and she cut me off.

"It's not cancer. It's pre-cancer. You can get a lumpectomy and remove it completely." I asked, "How is this possible?" She explained that their labs got a different result than the original lab.

It caught me so off guard that I couldn't even feel relief. I'd been through a month of hell. I'd put my family through a month of hell. I'd just started to get used to the idea of losing my breast, of learning to accept a new body, of understanding the risks to my life. Instead of feeling relieved, I was pissed. And confused.

I called the lab that did the original diagnosis, and they said they were standing by their recommendation. "Cancer's cancer," the woman on the other end quipped. "And it's cancer."

Two weeks later I went in for the lumpectomy. After all the preparation and planning, this felt like nothing. Snip, tug, done. Cancer, pre-cancer, whatever it was, it was out of my body.

That's how I ended 2014. I was cancer-free. My back was healing and I was determined to take note of the lessons these challenges presented.

Now I have a fermata tattooed on my left inner arm. It's the musical symbol for pause, and it's forever etched on to my skin to remind me of a lesson I can't afford to forget.

Sometimes it feels as if life is like water slipping through our hands and we have to scramble to catch it all before it's gone. But our scrambling actually has the opposite effect. We think we're drinking it all in before it can get away, but we're really just splashing it out in our rush to have it all. Sometimes the best thing we can do is to take a break and let the waters calm around us. Sip slowly.

Once the waters are calm we can stop worrying about what we have to do and start worrying about what we want to do. This is why my fermata curves over an olive branch tattoo. It's to remind me that what I am after is peace, not the appearance of success. It's a reminder to just fucking stop every once in a while. To just listen. Is this a place I want to be? Am I living a peaceful life? Is my life going in the right direction right now?

Just because you can do something doesn't mean you should do it. Your inner voice may shout or it may whisper. Either way, it's your job to hear it.

The message came through loud and clear: slow down and take stock. That's what I did. I couldn't run myself ragged anymore, and I had a career to build. My dad had been chatting with a colleague whose daughter was doing physical therapy work. He thought we should get to know one another because we might be good referral sources for each other's businesses. She invited me to come chat with her. "By the way," she said toward the end of our visit, "I have some available office space in this suite."

Space had been an issue. I had been seeing clients at my parents' house when I was recovering from the back injury. When I moved back home, I was still in a clamshell brace, and driving was uncomfortable. I had just rearranged my living room so I could bring clients into my home. I told her I wasn't really interested in office space. "But I'll take a look at it in case I run into anyone else who is looking," I offered.

As soon as I walked into the room I heard bells ringing. This was *my* space. It was exactly what I wanted. The room was welcoming but functional, with plenty of natural light. I could imagine the décor and the seating. I could see it all unfurl in front of me. "Could I bring my dog in here?" I asked. The Gods of Synchronicity had shined on me again.

I started my lease two weeks later. I continued to embrace the curvy path of this journey, and didn't get hung up on the fact that I'd just created a home office. Nearly every client comments on how welcoming and peaceful my office space feels. I can open the windows to let in fresh air and sunlight. Synchronicity!

Warning: Vehicle Makes Wide Right Turns

Once we've done the hard work of starting with self-compassion and taking stock to see what needs to change, it can be frustrating to realize our work isn't done. After all, it is difficult to let go of the common layers of protection that we wrap ourselves in: avoidance, denial, etc. It's often difficult to name our emotions and let them stop controlling us. It's challenging to make the decision to change some situations in our lives. Once we've worked through that, shouldn't we finally get what we want?

But the work still isn't done. Figuring out what we really want out of life is only half the battle. Once we know what we need, we still have to make it happen. That's what manifesting the life we want is all about.

My signs that there is work to be done:
- There is something I want in my life but don't have.
- A worry is weighing on my mind.

- I feel I have to know every possible outcome before I take the first step toward change.

The changes you want to make don't have to be huge. For example, as I write this I'm facing the need for manifestation myself. The building I've been using for office space was sold. Major renovations will disrupt my practice, and when it's all done my rent will triple. I have to find a new space.

Finding this space two years ago was a sign to me that I was on the right path. It fell into my life at just the right moment, and I suppose losing it could be viewed as a bad omen, a sign that things are going off track, the start of a spiral into negative self-talk and despair.

Instead, I know with 100 percent certainty that the right solution will present itself. Do I know how? No. I don't know what space I will find. I don't know how I will find it. I don't know what street it will be on or how it will affect my business.

Manifesting does not mean trying to micromanage yourself into paralysis. Manifesting does not mean waiting until everything is perfect before making a move. Manifesting means sending the message out into the Universe. It means being patient and attentive. Wait and stay alert. Trust that things will go the way they are meant to go, but don't leave it all up to chance. Recognize that action is imperative and be open so you see the opportunities.

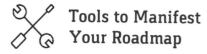 Tools to Manifest Your Roadmap

There's a four-step process to manifesting.

Step 1: Identify what you want.

This can be harder than it sounds. Sometimes what you think you want isn't the real root desire. Maybe you identify a want for more money, so you decide that what you want is a better-paying job. It could actually be that what you want is a job that is more satisfying so you stop spending all your money on material things that aren't making you happy. Maybe you decide you want a new car, but not just any car. You want a Tesla. Ask yourself why. What will you get from having a new Tesla? Is it attention you are seeking? Is it approval from others or the need to belong? You may come to realize that the Tesla isn't the answer. *What do you really need to manifest to fulfill the root of your needs?* Sometimes you think you want things because other people or the world around you has implied that you need them. Identifying what you want requires some reflection and thought. Once you've identified what you *really* want, the next steps become a lot easier and more fulfilling.

Step 2: Have absolute faith that it will work out when it is meant to work out.

This is the hardest part for most people. Once you've identified something you want in the world, a chorus of doubt seems to rise up from within—and sometimes from the outside as well. This is particularly true if what you decide you want doesn't align with what other people think you should want.

Maybe you've decided what you really want is a creative career that allows you to set your own hours. But your family is convinced that what you need is a stable nine-to-five. They are going to give you lots of reasons to doubt things will work out as you voice your new desire.

Even when you have support, your internal voice can tell you that what you want will never happen, that you're hoping for something you don't deserve, that you're being impractical, or that bad things always happen to you so that this too will be a disappointment.

You have to silence these voices. You have to really, truly believe that things will work out in time. That you deserve for them to work out. This isn't a magic wand. You don't get to snap your fingers and bring forth a new car because you've decided that's what you want. After drilling down into the root of that desire, then have faith it will come in the form it is meant to appear. In other words, the car may not come when you first ask for it. But then low and behold, your garage floods when a water main breaks. If you already had that new car it would have had a lot of water damage. The right car comes to you two weeks later. Just when it was supposed to all along.

Step 3: Take action.

Unfortunately, there aren't any magic genies in life. You don't get to wish for something, rub the lamp the right way, and sit back and enjoy. Instead, you have to work for it. Every day. Every week. Every month. Every year. This is the long game.

Whatever it is you have put into the Universe will come back to you, but you have to start taking steps to make it happen. Think of it like a garden. It's important to plant the seed, but you also have to take out the weeds, provide water, and make sure it is planted in a place with adequate sunlight.

The want alone is not enough. You have to also create the environment in which it can become a reality. So, if you want to grow sunflowers, don't plant the seeds under a shade tree.

Another very important, and often unspoken action that must be taken is to take the time to feel what it will be like when the manifestation becomes a reality. Feel as if you've already gotten the car or the job or the partner. The Universe requires more than words. It requires the energy of the feelings you are putting out in order to give back. Remember, the Law of Attraction is not about thinking about something and getting it. It is all about the *energy* you are putting into the Universe through your thoughts, emotions and actions!

Step 4: Let go of how it will happen.

Some people are really good planners. They have a goal and they work backwards to set subgoals until they have a plan. Their plans are mapped out for months at a time. They color code their to-do lists and stay focused and on the job. They have a plan in mind every step of the way and have contingency plans for everything that might go wrong. This can be great (though it can also be exhausting and stifling), but it is not *manifesting*.

If you are manifesting the life you want, you have to let go of how it will happen. Just as you fiercely believe that things will end up the way they should, you must also give up the desire to control exactly how that need will be fulfilled. If you spend so much time trying to shape the outcome, you might miss the path that would get you where you need to go. Remember the end goal rather than imagining how it might happen.

You probably know the parable about a man and a flood. He is a man of faith, and before the floodwaters rose, he told those evacuating around him that he knew God would provide for him, so he wouldn't be evacuating. They left without him. Once the waters start to rise, a pair of late-evacuating neighbors come by in a boat and told him to hop in.

"No, God will provide for me," he told them. They went on without him. He prayed. As the waters rose even more, he climbed to the roof, still completely sure that God would take care of him. An emergency crew found the man on his roof and asked him to get in their boat.

"No," he replied, "God will provide for me." He prayed. The waters continued to rise. Finally, a helicopter hovered above him as the rescuers spotted him and urged him to climb aboard.

"No," he called out, "God will provide for me." He prayed. Still, the waters rose. He was climbing up his chimney, and his faith was wavering.

"God, I have been a faithful man. I have put all my trust in you. How could you turn your back on me in my time of need?"

Then the sky split open and a voice boomed down.

"I gave you warnings to evacuate and sent two boats and a helicopter. What more do you want?!"

The help we get might not look the way we expect it to look. That doesn't mean it is any less valuable. In fact, by being willing to be guided down unexpected paths we can end up in the most amazing places, living lives we never expected to live.

Throughout my life, there have been times when things just seemed to work. When I owned my eco-consulting firm, I knew I needed office space to keep my company afloat, but I didn't have the money to rent.

I had gotten to the point where I had grown out of my home office. I was carrying an inventory of eco-friendly cleaning products and other supplies to help people "green" their homes, and I was bringing someone in to work with me, so I needed actual office space. However, I wasn't bringing in a lot of money yet, so I couldn't afford anything.

Remember, the trick to manifesting is not only to envision what you want, but also to imagine the feeling you will have when you get it and, most importantly, to let go of any attachment to how what you want is going to come about. In other words, if I had gone into this process by saying, "Here's how I'm going to get this," I would have been *blocking out all of the infinite other possible ways that it could come.* You have to stay completely open to how the outcome is going to materialize.

I let it be known to anybody and everybody that I was looking for office space. Within 48 hours my father told me that he'd found me space with an accounting firm that had extra, unused offices. They were willing to let me use a 300-square-foot space for free, indefinitely! That's how I manifested my Green It! office.

I have many manifestation stories but my favorite happened when my daughter Dylan had been accepted to two schools: Denver University and Santa Clara

University. I had gone to Denver University, but that wasn't why I wanted her to go there. Dawn, my dear friend and roommate from college still lived in Denver.

I felt that if Dylan went to D.U. Dawn would be there to offer her a safe place. If Dylan had problems, she'd have someone to turn to. If she ever went to the ER, there would be someone who would wait with her until I got there. In Santa Clara there was nobody. That's why I was hoping she would pick Denver, and when she didn't, I was concerned that she would be all the way out in California alone.

I knew what I really needed was peace about this situation. I had no idea how I would get that, but I imagined that condition and let go of the circumstances that would make it arise.

That summer I took her to Santa Clara for orientation. Dylan and I went to the university clinic to ask about getting her prescriptions filled and delivered. The clinic used a pharmacy two towns over to deliver the medications to the campus for pick-up. When I got back to St. Louis I called the pharmacy and arranged to get her prescriptions transferred from our local pharmacy. The next day I got a phone call from the California pharmacy to say one of them wasn't ready to be refilled, which was a nice but unnecessary courtesy call because I just wanted the prescriptions on file for the next refill. As the pharmacist was talking to me, she said, "I grew up not far from where you live." We started playing what's commonly known as "Jewish geography," and I asked her maiden name.

I was sitting in my office of Green It! and when she told me her name, I yelled, "Shut the fuck up!" so loud that the accountant on the other side of the wall clearly heard every word I said.

It turns out that this pharmacist was my cousin! I didn't know her, but I was good friends with her two brothers. She was quite a bit younger, so we had never come across one another in childhood.

My cousin was one of many pharmacists working at this pharmacy two towns away, and she only worked part-time. Yet she was the pharmacist that was given my daughter's prescription to work on. Not only was Dylan not alone in California, she had family there! My cousin invited her over for a Friday night dinner. Dylan took the train and when she got off, the entire family was standing on the platform with signs welcoming her. They took her home and fed her and made her feel welcome. From then on, I knew she had a soft place to land (though luckily, she never needed to use it) if anything went really wrong.

My peace came in a way I could never have predicted or asked for in a million years of guessing the outcome.

When you recognize what it is you *really* want and let go of how it will look when you get it, you'll find that the energy you channel into making it a reality is rarely wasted.

Course Corrections

Appreciating the Beauty Along the Way

The struggle to fully accept myself and love myself for who I am, inside and out, is something I share with almost everyone I counsel or coach. This theme is a constant in my own life and has led me to two of the most powerful tools I use in my Body Positive practice: Health at Every Size® and Intuitive Eating. Together these concepts have helped both me and the people I counsel move toward a goal most of us thought we could never achieve: radical self-acceptance.

The path to self-acceptance is paved in the scars that I see in the mirror. I have had six surgeries between my groin and my armpits. Two C-sections. Two biopsies. A lumpectomy. A breast reduction. A scar from where they had tried to do the arthroscopic appendectomy that would have left a small scar, but they'd had to go in for the big one instead. My body has been through a lot, and it wears the marks in dents and lines that ripple across it. Standing in that mirror, I realize that my body has done a hell of a job keeping me alive, keeping me strong, and bringing me to this point. It is a metaphorical road map of my life.

I've been every size from 4 to 14, and even though I now identify as a body positive therapist, the road here was a bumpy one, and I still find myself veering off course now and then.

From puberty through college I had a tiny waist and curvy hips, and I somehow convinced myself I was fat and unattractive. That's a common tale for women facing the pressures to constantly look thinner, smaller, *better*. The next part of my tale is even more common.

I had a few pounds from my first pregnancy that I just couldn't shake. After the next pregnancy, there were a few more pounds. And after 18 months on steroids, I had many more pounds. When I got GBS, I remember lying in bed, paralyzed, thinking, *Well, hopefully I'll at least lose a little weight.* How messed up is that? I was fighting to get my body back to working order and I was thinking that losing some weight could be a good thing to come of it!

When I got the new cancer diagnosis that meant I wouldn't be getting a mastectomy after all, part of me was disappointed because I wouldn't be removing fat from my belly for the breast reconstruction. That's right. I was disappointed I didn't have cancer. Because I wanted the fat out of my stomach. How could someone think such a thing?

I tried every diet program. Weight Watchers®. Jenny Craig®. I injected myself with shots that were supposed to dissolve fat. I tried being vegetarian. I tried going gluten-free. I went Paleo for three years.

What started as cruel thoughts about my own body as a teen escalated in adulthood. When I was back on the dating scene after my divorce, I'd see guy's profiles on dating websites. Under the description of what they were seeking, they'd have one of two boxes marked: "athletic and toned" or "slender." Why even bother? At this point I've spoken with enough women and men to know my story is all too common. I now realize there is hardly a person out there that does not struggle with body issues. But that doesn't make it hurt any less to be uncomfortable in your own skin, to be unhappy with your appearance and to put yourself through the ringer trying to literally shape yourself into someone else's version of beauty.

I'd been through the literal paralysis and recovery from GBS and the figurative paralysis of moving out of the rut of my marriage. I'd built up a career only to see it crumble with the housing market and then started all over again... and again! I'd picked myself up from the bottom of depression and held my head high as I found my path in life and got on it. I'd learned to face challenging times with a positive attitude, take responsibility for my own life, and manifest the opportunities I needed to thrive.

But somehow I still hadn't figured out radical self-acceptance, how to accept and love myself for who I was.

Growing up, it can feel like our bodies are betraying us. When I was young, my great-grandmother would always say, "you're six o'clock—straight up and down" or "you're a tall glass of water." Then, around puberty I started rounding out. In high school I had the tiniest waist and an hourglass figure. Looking back at pictures, I see a young woman with a smoking hot body, but that wasn't what I saw at the time.

I was 12 and at summer camp when I first got my period. I was mortified and didn't want to tell anyone, so I stuffed toilet paper in my underwear. My mom had never had "the talk" with me, so I only knew what was going on from talking with my friends. They weren't the most reliable source of information. On day three I sucked it up and went to the infirmary and told the nurse. I asked her not to, but she immediately called my mom. I was trying to play it cool.

"Don't be scared, honey!" my mom said, and something about her voice triggered me and I burst into tears. All I wanted was to stop walking around with toilet paper shoved between my legs, but now it was a thing, and I felt embarrassed by my body, lonely and scared.

My curly hair also made me feel like an outlier in a school full of WASPs with straight, blonde hair. I worked so hard to tame that hair. I wanted it to be straight so badly. It was stupid of me to want to get rid of something so uniquely me. But to this day, I've noticed how strong women in movies or on TV never have curly hair. In a movie called *The Women*—where literally the entire cast is women, Meg Ryan has the cutest, curliest hair, and I was so excited to see her play this part. But then one day she goes to kick some ass, and her hair from that scene on is poker straight. Juliana Marguiles from *The Good Wife* has gorgeous curly hair, but she wears a straight hair wig on the show. The curly-haired women are always the goofy sidekicks, never to be taken seriously. I liked my curly hair, but damn it, I wanted to fit in and be taken seriously!

One of the themes throughout my life is how hard I've worked to feel like my body was acceptable. I used to feel like I had to change myself to fit societal expectations.

Maybe I got that message because no matter where I turned, some voice has always been screaming at me about what I'm supposed to look like, how I'm supposed to dress, and the way I'm supposed to act. Whether it came from the other moms at my daughters' school or the advertisements for shampoo featuring yet another shiny-haired blonde, I've had no shortage of motivators to change to fit my surroundings. Those surroundings had overwhelmingly taught me that I'm the odd one out, the one in need of the most changing.

Over the years my pendulum of weight loss efforts have swung every which way. The most recent and final effort was trying the Paleo diet. I didn't ease myself into it. I just woke up one day and cut grains, dairy, and sugar from my diet completely. It was a challenge, but I thrive in situations where I can feel the pride of accomplishment. It was like winning a little award every day when I stuck to the plan.

I lost 40 pounds! Of course, this was combined with the stress of the bankruptcy, the side effects of the migraine medicine and not eating for days. Whenever someone asked me how I was making the change, I'd tell them about the diet, and they'd always say, "But don't you miss the food?"

I'd laugh and tell them, "Not at all." I'd point to how healthy this way of eating made me feel (when what it really made me feel was that I had some control in my life at a time when I felt that was lacking). What's a piece of cake that lasts 10 minutes compared to a healthy body that lasts a lifetime? I meant that at first, but then I did

beth koritz

start to miss the cake. I went to a music festival one year and still managed to plan all my meals around the diet. I packed, planned, and prepped. I was determined to stay on the path that was getting me the results I had been seeking for so long.

I spent hours prepping those meals and tons of money bringing fresh food to an outdoor festival. I had to run back and forth to a gas station to add ice to the cooler and keep it all from spoiling. I missed half the damn music because I spent the entire trip worrying about what and how I could eat! I now know this is disordered eating at its finest!

I went back to the festival the next year and decided I wasn't going to do it again. I wasn't going to waste all that time and money when there was a food vendor selling absolutely delicious slices of pizza for a couple of bucks just feet away from the music.

That's how it started. I would have an off day now and then. I'd have a pizza one night and be back to the diet the next. It wasn't like vegetarianism where an ethical line kept it all or nothing. For a while after the festival, I kept up Paleo most of the time. I might have a slice of cake to celebrate a special event, but most of the time I still stuck to the restrictions.

I wasn't willing to give up all those accomplishments, all those pounds lost, but it was still about restriction. I was worried more about what I looked like than how I felt, and that's ridiculous!

I no longer eat to force my body into a certain shape or size. That's what had been wrong with all those failed diet programs. In Weight Watchers meetings, we never talked about what choices made us feel good, what allowed us to be strong and happy. All we ever talked about was numbers. How many points had I eaten that day? How many pounds had I lost? How many inches was I down? I became a walking algebra problem.

Going Paleo had its benefits. It taught me to pay attention to how food made my body feel, but ultimately, I was making sacrifices for the sake of sacrifices, for the sake of maintaining my 40-pound weight loss rather than feeding my body well. By the way, I look at pictures of myself back then and I don't recognize myself. It was obviously not the authentic me.

I thank the Universe for the day I learned about Body Positive Psychology, Intuitive Eating, and Health at Every Size®.

Intuitive Eating is about being mindful and listening when your body tells you what it needs. When it is hungry and when it is full. What nutrients it is short on is what you will crave. Identifying when you are eating but not hungry and asking yourself why. *Am I bored? Am I eating for comfort that I am not getting elsewhere? Am I eating my feelings?* If I'm bored, my goal is to get busy doing something more productive. If I need comfort I will reach out to a friend. If it is to drown out feelings, I know that these feelings need to be validated and honored, not covered in food.

Intuitive Eating has no restrictions. Restricting food only leads to binge eating. If nothing is off limits there is no need to overeat. If I want a piece of chocolate cake, I will have it, enjoying every morsel that passes my lips. Because I am paying attention to what my body is telling me, I will stop when I am no longer hungry, knowing I don't have to gorge on the cake today because I can have some more tomorrow if I choose to.

Side note: I have been telling you what I will do under all these circumstances, when in reality these are the things I strive to do. Being human means it does not always happen that way, and that is okay, too. There is no self-recrimination or punishment. There is nothing here to forgive!

I could write a whole book about Intuitive Eating but that has already been done and done brilliantly. I hope that you will find the book *Intuitive Eating: A Revolutionary Program that Works* by Evelyn Tribole MS, RD and Elyse Resch, MS, RDN, FADA, CEDRD as helpful and life-changing as I have.

Health at Every Size® (HAES) is based on the premise that a person's size is not indicative of their health. Many size 20 women are healthier than some size 2 women. HAES is based on the idea that health should be judged by metabolic levels i.e. heart rate, cholesterol, blood sugars, etc., not on a number on a scale or BMI (see the Resource section for a link to an article about how absurd BMI is as a scale of health). It is freeing for woman to learn that there is not always a direct correlation between size and health.

There are so many Body Positive resources available. I encourage you to check them out. Hundreds, if not thousands, of people on social media share the message of radical self-acceptance. I am excited that we are at a time in history when society is judging women less for their bodies and more for what is within. But we still have a very long way to go.

One thing I do, and suggest to clients, is to fill my Instagram and Facebook feeds with inspiration and knowledge. I will instantly block, hide or delete any person, company, or hashtag that does not support my feeling good about myself and my journey. I'm happy to know that by the time you read this, so many more wonderful resources will be out there.

Even with all of this recently found knowledge that I have just shared, I had over 50 years of built-in thought and behavior mechanisms that had been drilled into me by societal expectations, the diet industry, and product messages. As a counselor who now helps people face their own body-image challenges and insecurities, I relate to my clients because these issues still pop up for me. After living with them for five decades, I don't think it's reasonable to think that they will ever completely disappear, and that is okay. The difference is that now I know how to manage them. I still hear a tiny voice in my mind groan when I notice my clothes are fitting a little tighter. On the other hand, I give myself an internal cheer when I order the delicious cake and enjoy every crumb of it until I am full.

When I was working toward certification in Body Positive Psychology, I asked one of the instructors if I could really help someone else through their problems if I hadn't fixed all of my own. She told me I had to ask myself some key questions: *Am I treating myself with love? Am I eating with love?* From there, I can move into self-compassion and remember that I am human. No one can let go of all of that baggage and societal conditioning overnight. It's a process, and we will make mistakes. Questioning our choices and our body may be inevitable. The most important thing is that we have a toolbox with supporters, and positive thoughts when the questions arise.

When I ask myself if I am healthy now, I have to find the answer that is based on what I love about myself and how I feel physically and emotionally, not the one based on some diet plan's script of numbers.

It's okay to ask the questions, but now I've found a set of answers that don't send me into a shame spiral that ends with self-condemnation. I've broken free of that script. That's what gives me the power to truly take care of myself.

The big takeaway - loving who we are as human beings underpins every other measure of success. The lesson I learned over and over again in my life was that I was the common factor in everything that happened to me—and everything I made happen. We can't base our sense of worth on the body we inhabit, the job we have, or the balance in our bank account. Who you are as a human being transcends all of those typical markers of identity and success. Who you are as a human being is rooted deeper and lasts longer, and it is there no matter what.

Be aware of your surroundings

If you are always striving to be your best, most authentic self, you are constantly touching base with that internal identity, the one that can't be changed by gaining or losing 10 pounds, getting a promotion or losing a job, winning the lottery or going into bankruptcy.

I often ask my clients to make a list of their qualities. It's funny because when I say that, they always ask the same question: "The good *and* the bad?" It's funny to me because my intention is always the good. If it's bad, it's not really a *quality*, is it? The word itself implies that it has worth and purpose. If they bring up the bad, though, I say "Sure." I want them to take stock of how they see themselves.

When clients show me this list, it's amazing how often I will find "good" qualities written in the "bad" column. They perceive strengths as weaknesses. This is especially true for my female clients. They'll say they are "bossy." Introverts will say that they "aren't social." A lot of my work is getting them to flip this script. "You say you're bossy, but do you take on leadership roles well? Should that be on the good side?" "You say you're awkward in social settings, but are you a good listener? Should that be in the other column?" Even if the bad remains on the list, there is almost always a connected quality that balances it out.

Another interesting pattern to these lists is how often the "good" qualities are external measures of success. People will write that they are good athletes, that they make a lot of money, that they are pretty, or that they bake delicious cakes. Rarely do they write about qualities that reflect what kind of human being they are, the kinds of things that are true no matter the circumstances. I almost never see clients list themselves as "loyal" or "kind." They reflect on what they're good at doing rather than what they're good at being.

If you blow out your knee, you won't be a good athlete anymore. If you lose your job, you won't have as much money. Circumstances can change, but who you are underneath it all does not. You can always be loyal, kind, caring, compassionate, and funny. These are not superficial or dependent qualities—they are *your authentic you.*

 ## Tools for the Journey to You

If you want to find out who your authentic self is, here are some steps you can take.

Step 1: Make a list.

Make a list of the qualities you have. Try not to think in a binary of good or bad. List the attributes that make you who you are. If you are having trouble coming up with any, think about the way you interact with the world. What would your friends say about you? What would the person who has known you the longest say about you? What would your co-workers say about you? What would your dog say about you? What would someone observing you from a distance say about you? How do the actions you take every day shape the way you move through life?

Step 2: Identify what weaknesses may really be strengths or neutral qualities.

Look at that list. I'm willing to bet that some negative qualities snuck in there. Maybe you wrote that you were messy or anxious or conceited or petty.

Start by figuring out which are actually positive qualities that you've been conditioned to downplay or reject. If you're "bossy," ask yourself if you are actually confident. If you're "messy," ask yourself if you are actually creative.

Plenty of qualities feel like negatives but are actually just neutral parts of existing in the world. Maybe you don't necessarily like the fact that you are a picky eater or quiet, but if they aren't negatively impacting who you are and what you want in life, there's no need to cast them as negative attributes.

Maybe some of these are truly negative. That means you should ask yourself what you're going to do to change them. Start with acceptance. Accept everything about who you are as a condition of being in this moment, and then ask if that reality is helping you be the best version of yourself. If the answer is no, then working to change those aspects of yourself is part of the process. It doesn't mean you stop accepting who you are today. You can have full acceptance of that aspect's current existence without deciding to accept it as a permanent feature.

Step 3: Practice self-care.

Once you have taken an honest, full account of who you are, you must begin any changes with self-care. If you found positive qualities that you want to bring forward in your life or negative traits that you want to change, the first step is the same: care for yourself. You cannot grow a garden in toxic soil, and you do not become the person you want to be through negativity and shame.

What does self-care look like to you? Is it finding five minutes each morning to meditate or quietly enjoy a cup of coffee? Is it pampering yourself with a massage or making sure you find time to be outdoors? As a therapist, there are inevitably days that I bring a client's tragic story home in my thoughts. I have learned that downtime is a must for me. In addition to having daily time to turn off my mind (which could just be watching a TV show I enjoy) I need to create, so I always have a couple of knitting and crochet projects next to my couch. I have also learned that traveling, to completely detach, is critical for my wellbeing. So, I make sure that every three to four months I get away, even if it's just driving a few hours away for a weekend.

I found the Body Positivity philosophy and the Intuitive Eating/HAES movements just as I turned 50. It was a wake-up call. I think it's a shame that so many of us have to get to our 40s or 50s before we feel secure enough to shed societal expectations and look for another way to see ourselves.

Once you realize who you authentically are and approach that existence with compassion and self-care, it's a lot easier to realize that you'll be spending the rest of your days with this person. Instead of trying to berate, shame, or cajole yourself into becoming something you are not, radically embrace who you are. Often, the world will surprise you by doing the same.

Tools to Create your Resilience Road Map

- Focus on what you can do and can control. Do not dwell on the negativity, the pain, or the things you can't do and can't control.
- Be willing and able to take responsibility for your actions, thoughts, and emotions. Do not blame others for what is yours to own.
- Make the choices that best serve your authentic self and take action without the worry of being judged.
- Define your success by your levels of happiness and fulfillment, not by dollar signs *and not by anyone else's definition.*
- Allow yourself to want what you want, both the possible and impossible, without getting hung up on how they will happen.
- Be open to embracing and using humor because, as the saying goes, "If you don't laugh, you will cry."
- Be open to every opportunity, no matter where it comes from. Do not limit yourself by

thinking you know where it will come from or where it will lead. This closes the door to all of the other infinite possibilities the Universe has to offer.

- If you find yourself in an environment that stifles your ability to be positive, change your environment (or at least try like hell to).
- Practice good self-care. Get enough sleep. Eat what your body needs. Find the time to be quiet enough to hear your inner voice. Be active. Practice self-compassion.
- Ask for help. Remember, this is a sign of strength, not weakness!

Finally:

Look at your life's experiences:

What was the lesson/positive that came out of them?

How are you able to focus on what you can control?

Think about examples along your journey where you have found the lesson or focused on what you could control without actively realizing that was what you were doing.

When you look back at these examples, can you identify what tools you used to get through these experiences?

P.S. Congratulations! You have already been successfully using this road map without even realizing it! Rock On!

Resources

I find these books (and one article) helpful and often suggest them to my clients and friends. I hope you also find them useful.

- *Body Kindness: Transform Your Health from the Inside Out--and Never Say Diet Again* by Rebecca Scritchfield, RDN
- *Embody: Learning to Love Your Unique Body* by Connie Sobczak
- *Everything You Need is Right Here* by Kimberly V. Schneider, M.Ed., J.D., LPC
- *Health at Every Size: The Surprising Truth about Your Weight* by Linda Bacon, PhD
- *Intuitive Eating: A Revolutionary Program that Works, Third Edition* by Evelyn Tribole, MS, RD and Elyse Resch, MS, RD, FADA, CEDRD
- *Self-Compassion: The Proven Power of Being Kind to Yourself* by Kristin Neff, PhD
- *Top 10 Reasons Why The BMI Is Bogus*

  https://npr.org/templates/story/story.php?storyId=106268439

Thank you for joining me on my resilience road!
Please leave a review on Amazon to let other readers
know how the book touched you.
To contact me and find more wonderful resources
please visit my websites:
bethkoritz.com
resilienceroad.com

and join my exploration on Facebook and Instagram
@bethkoritzlpc

Lastly, are you looking for
inspiration or to inspire,
support or to be supportive,
role-models or to be a role-model?

If so, please
JOIN OUR FACEBOOK COMMUNITY
@resilience road - exploring your authentic life path

About the Author

What do you get when you've been through divorce, paralysis, and a late-in-the-game career change? Ask Beth Koritz, and she'll tell you that what you get is perspective and the chance to live your life without fear that you're breaking someone else's rules.

Following a winding path through several careers, relationships and illnesses, Beth found her purpose as a licensed professional counselor after graduating with her master's degree at the age of 50.

Beth believes that the key to a happy, joy-filled life is getting to know your authentic self and striving to be the best version of her. This self-exploration entails being open to all the Universe has to offer, the willingness to take responsibility for all of your thoughts, actions and emotions, and learning self-compassion. Her first-hand experiences taught her to pause and sit in the quiet, allowing her inner voice to guide her personal journey.

215

Beth's areas of expertise center around the issues she is most passionate about. These include quieting the critical inner voice, body image, Intuitive Eating, Health at Every Size®, creating solutions and opportunities, and working through depression and/or anxiety. She finds joy working with clients who truly want to feel better about themselves and their journeys, improve their outlook, their relationships, and move forward from difficult times.

Beth lives in St. Louis, MO in a 100-year-old house where she uses her creativity and her love for natural materials to make a home that is unique in function and design. She enjoys her downtime surrounded by yarn, hooks, and needles with her mini aussie-doodle, Cassidy Blue, by her side.

Beth's pride and joy are her two daughters, who are her inspiration and daily reminder of what matters most. In her spare time, you'll find Beth attending concerts, visiting the mountains, and dreaming of living part-time in Colorado.

Currently, Beth is creating a coaching program based on the strategies and philosophies she weaves throughout *resilience road*. For more information: resilienceroad.com

62415158R00138

Made in the USA
Columbia, SC
02 July 2019